Drover's Dog

by the same author with Ray Owen

OLD ENGLISH SHEEPDOGS

DROVER'S DOG

SYLVIA WOODS
illustrated by Gavin Rowe

ff
faber and faber

First published in 1983
by Faber and Faber Limited
3 Queen Square London WC1N 3AU
Printed in Great Britain by
Redwood Burn Ltd Trowbridge Wiltshire

British Library Cataloguing in Publication Data

Woods, Sylvia
Drover's dog.
I. Title
823'.914[J] PZ7

ISBN 0-571-11993-X

Contents

After bringing their cattle to Smithfield Market in London, drovers in the seventeenth century would travel home by coach and leave their dogs to find their own way back. Many of these dogs had to cover long distances in order to get home; some of them came from Scotland or Wales, others came from the north or the west of England. The dogs walked back the way they had come, calling at farms and inns where they had stopped on the journey into London. The farmers and innkeepers gave them food and water and allowed them to rest before continuing their journey home.

Drover's Dog is the story of a dog who had to make this journey by himself.

1 : Alone in London

Smithfield was full of dogs; Bobtail had never seen so many. Most of them had short black and white coats, pointed muzzles, small feet and feathery tails. Bobtail had a long grey coat and a huge white head, big furry feet and no tail at all; this made him look like a bear from the back. There weren't many dogs like him at the market, and young William Garson, who walked beside his father as they drove their cattle with Bobtail's help, felt very proud of him.

Bobtail did not look like the other dogs, but he felt the same as they did. Like them, he had cracked pads and aching feet and he was very hungry. They were all drovers' dogs who had helped their masters to bring hundreds of cattle from all parts of the country to the great London market at Smithfield for the Michaelmas slaughter. Every year, in the late autumn, cattle had to be killed because there was not enough grass or other sorts of food to feed them through the winter. The meat was preserved in salt so that it would last until the late spring without going bad. Fresh meat during the winter months was a great luxury. Even King Charles and his courtiers at Whitehall had to eat salted meat sometimes.

William and his father had risen early that morning. They had been staying at an inn in the village of Paddington, but they left while it was still dark to collect their cattle, which were pastured in a large field behind the inn. With Bobtail to help them, they drove the cattle towards the sunrise. They saw the great tower and long roof of St. Paul's Cathedral sharp against the pale yellow of the sky, and then they were in the hubbub of Smithfield Market.

The noise of geese and cattle and dogs astounded William, but his father, who attended the market regularly, took it for granted. He found the butcher he always dealt with and began talking business.

William, at a word from his father, left them and set out to explore. He slipped unnoticed through the crowd of drovers, apprentices, housewives buying tallow for candles, horse dealers, pedlars and beggars. He was too young to be of interest to pickpockets, and recruiting officers from London's army passed him without a second glance. Every large town and city had to maintain a small army, ready to defend the country in war. These armies were called the trained bands. Just now King Charles was quarrelling with Parliament and the trained bands of London were on Parliament's side. William, visiting London for the first time in his life, knew nothing about such problems. He was only interested in watching a group of jugglers and tumblers who had turned up to entertain the crowd.

Bobtail stayed with his master, but when the cattle had been penned, and Mr. Garson went off in search of William, he was left alone. A delicious smell of fresh raw meat was coming from the shambles where the beasts were being slaughtered. He trotted off, full of hope, towards an area where a butcher and his assistants were hard at work. A huge piece of cow's stomach, rejected by the butchers, came flying through the air to land at his feet. Bobtail leaned forward eagerly to take it, but an enormous dog swiped him aside and took his prize from under his nose. He was left rolling over and over among the refuse beneath the butchers' benches.

He picked himself up and shook some of the interesting-smelling wetness out of his coat. Above him, the butchers continued their work. Fifty yards away, the large dog was devouring what Bobtail had hoped would be his breakfast. It was not going to be as easy as it had seemed at first. He might have to fight for his food, unless he got in before anyone else noticed. He looked round, and saw a red splodge of meat at the butcher's feet. Bobtail edged towards it and lifted a paw. He was not quite quick enough. There was an oath and he was kicked aside by an unfriendly boot. Obviously that piece had belonged to the butcher.

By the end of the morning, Bobtail had learned how to fend for himself. You had to be quick, and you had to be prepared to fight. He also learnt that if you were still a puppy, and this was your first visit to Smithfield, you took care to avoid older, experienced dogs who approached stiff-legged with hackles raised. Most of the puppies who came to Smithfield for the first time had an older dog with them who stood while the youngster ate. Until coming to London, Bobtail had always had his father, seven-year-old Watchboy, to keep him company. But two weeks before the herd was due to set out for Smithfield, Watchboy had broken his leg. In spite of the clever splint Mr. Garson had made, anyone could see that the dog was not fit to go. Nell, Watchboy's mother, was still alive, but her working life was over and nine-month-old Bobtail was the only dog left.

With only a puppy to help him, Mr. Garson had decided to take William as well. His mother had been doubtful, for William was only ten, but he himself was delighted. Walking with his father all the way to London, he passed through towns and villages and countryside he had never expected to see so soon. At the end of the journey, Mr. Garson had to admit that both William and Bobtail had done very well.

After selling their cattle the Garsons remained in London for a few days. William went about with his father and the puppy was usually at their heels. Sometimes Bobtail went off to the market and rolled and played and fought with the other dogs who arrived daily as new herds were driven in. When he was hungry, there was always food in the shambles. One morning, in the middle of a scrap with some other young dogs, he heard William's voice calling him. He ran off at once. William and Mr. Garson were standing beside a coach, plainly having an argument. Mr.

Garson took Bobtail, faced him away from the market and said firmly, "Home, boy!"

William threw his arms around Bobtail, for once not grumbling about how smelly he was, and looked imploringly at his father. Mr. Garson shook his head and lifted his son into the coach. Bobtail was left behind, while the coachman whipped up the horses and a rebellious and tearful William was borne away down the street.

Bobtail tried to keep up with the coach, but almost immediately he became mixed up with other traffic, and a rearing horse kicked him hard in the ribs. By this time, William's coach had disappeared, but Bobtail refused to give up and ran on, limping as he went. William was in that coach and he and William had never been separated before.

He stopped at last to have a drink from a gutter beneath one of the houses. London gutter water tasted much stronger than the water in the streams at home. It did not quench the thirst so well, but there was nothing else. Then he ran on again, but there was no quick way through the confusing jumble of horses' hooves, carriage wheels and human feet. The pain in his side was growing worse as he ran. He sat down miserably, with his back against a wall. The afternoon was closing in. A murky fog was making its way up from the river, twisting along the streets. Bobtail curled up against the wall and slept.

He woke to find that the fog had lifted, the sky was clear and a red sun shone cosily. Shouts reached his ears, distant at first, but coming nearer. He turned his head to see a crowd of boys, older than William, running down the street. They were all waving clubs and laughing and jostling. He sat bolt upright and tried to push himself into the wall.

"No bishops!" cried one boy, who seemed to be their leader.

The others echoed him. "No bishops! No bishops!"

Shopkeepers in the street were closing the shutters over their shopfronts earlier than usual. They were afraid the apprentices would start looting their shops.

The boys passed on, and Bobtail relaxed and lay down, nose on forepaws. Just then, two more boys came out of a clockmaker's shop further up the street and ran to join the others.

"No bishops!" yelled one, a ginger-haired boy of about fourteen.

"No bish—hang and drat!" The second boy tripped over Bobtail's feet and fell. Bobtail leaped up with a cry of pain and stood with his head down, rubbing his bruised nose between his two front paws.

The first boy stopped, came back and helped his companion to his feet.

"You've hurt the dog," he said.

"Confound the dog. What about me?" The second boy picked up his cap, rammed it on his head and ruefully examined a great tear in his stockings.

ran with the two apprentices when they escaped from their master, and barked when they shook their clubs and shouted "No bishops!"

This was a favourite cry of the apprentices. They agreed with those members of Parliament who wanted to do without bishops and archbishops, and have ordinary ministers in charge of the Church. King Charles and his friend Archbishop Laud thought otherwise and this was one reason why the King was quarrelling with Parliament.

In the evening, Bobtail went back to the clockmaker's house, and at night he made his way to the small room where the two apprentices lay beneath their thin blankets, wearing all their clothes because the weather had turned so cold. He would jump on to the bed and warm them as he stretched his great furry body between theirs, and snore gently while the boys' talk ebbed and flowed above his head.

On the seventh day, the two boys missed their companion. The red November sun had set mistily that afternoon and a cold breeze blew in from the west. Bobtail stood outside the house with his big black nose turned towards it. The tall house with its shelter and companionship stood invitingly behind him, but Bobtail did not go in. Something in that fresh wind from the west stirred his homing instincts and he remembered another house, a long way away in the country, where a boy was waiting for him. As the memories came flooding back, he turned his back on the London house and set off with his bear-like shamble down the street towards the west.

2 : The Garsons come home

William climbed stiffly down from the coach and lifted his face to the November rain which was coming slantwise over the fields from the direction of the sea. Some money passed between his father and the driver. Then the coach lurched off, ploughing its way through the brown puddles and churned-up mud which, after three days of incessant rain, was all that was left of the Bridgwater road.

"Will!" Becky came running out to her brother. "Haven't you brought him back with you?"

"Father wouldn't let me."

"But he'll never get back on his own. All that way." Becky's eyes filled with tears.

"Father says that if Bobtail can't find his way, it'll show he's no good for the work. But he *is* good, Becky. He's marvellous with the cattle; it's bred in him. He's going to be like Watchboy. I wish you could have seen him."

"So do I," said Becky, pulling a face. "It isn't fair that only boys can go to London. I'll never get there and you'll be going every year now. If I'd been there, I'd have stayed behind and walked with Bobtail."

"Father wouldn't have let you," said William shortly. Not for worlds would he have told his sister how he had been lifted up and bundled into the coach when he had tried to argue with his father.

They walked up the path together and through the doorway into the living room. Mr. Garson was already pulling off his boots, and a meal was laid on the table, ready for the travellers.

When William came in, two dogs, stretched out in front of the fire, thumped their tails in greeting. Nell was seventeen years old and almost completely blind. She rose with difficulty and limped over to where William sat at the far end of the table, to have her ears stroked. Watchboy, who had a home-made splint firmly in place on his off-hind leg, made no attempt to rise from the pile of fresh rushes and sacking, but pricked his ears and wagged his tail all the harder to show how pleased he was to see William safely back.

While Mr. Garson told his wife the news of London, Becky waited on William and her father, fetching meat pies, oatcakes, apple tarts, and home-brewed beer. When she had finished serving them, she sat down beside William.

"He's only a baby," she said.

"A very big baby." William smiled as he thought of the enormous shaggy dog which had helped them drive the cattle to Smithfield. Then he grew serious again. "It was no good. The coach was very full. They grumbled when we got in and, anyway, Bobtail was absolutely filthy. You've no idea how dirty Smithfield is. And where they kill the cattle . . . you'd be sick. Bobtail had been rolling in it; you could smell him all over London."

"I know he's big, and I know his coat gets in a mess and he rolls in things, but he isn't a year old yet. Couldn't you have cleaned him up and come in another coach?"

"Only a few go to Bridgwater. We had a chance of a lift on this one and Father said we ought to take it because he felt rain was on the way and the road would get too bad for any more coaches to get through. That one we were on will be lucky if it gets to Bridgwater tonight without getting stuck."

"I wish Watchboy's leg had got better in time for him to go with Bobtail," said Becky.

Bobtail was very special to them both. To begin with, he was unlike any other cattle dog in the neighbourhood. His mother lived at Robert Ashe's farm across the fields. She was a short-coated, black and white bitch, very like Bobtail's father, Watchboy. She had produced two puppies in late February. One was just like herself; the other was Bobtail. He had been born without a tail, not even a stump. William and Becky, who had seen the puppies a week after they were born, christened him Bobtail, which was what the shepherds called all tailless dogs. His head was large and square and completely white. One eye was brown and the other was pale blue. His chest, belly and all four paws were white and the rest of his firm, stocky body was jet black. Robert Ashe had promised Mr. Garson a puppy, and William and Becky asked for Bobtail. So the strange little bundle without a tail came to live at their cottage when it was eight weeks old.

With the passing months, his short baby coat grew longer and shaggier. Soon his head hair was so long that it hid the blue eye and, as the black hair on his body and legs grew, it turned a beautiful shade of pale grey. By the time he was nine months old, he stood higher at the shoulder than his own mother, and was almost as tall as Watchboy.

Many of the farmers in the district said that Bobtail had the wrong build for a working dog. But Mr. Garson thought differently. He had met drovers from other parts of the country who used dogs like Bobtail, and they were reliable working dogs. They moved surprisingly quickly too, in spite of their size, and were very good with both sheep and cattle.

Bobtail was quick and intelligent, and easily learnt to follow Watchboy as a cattle dog. He was more excitable

and bouncy than Watchboy or Nell had ever been, but a word from Mr. Garson would always steady him down. When he wasn't working, he made a wonderful playmate for William and Becky.

When the time had come to leave for Smithfield, Watchboy was shut in the house and his dismal howls had accompanied William and his father for the first slow quarter of a mile of their journey. Bobtail was torn between wanting to move the cattle along, and wanting to go back and bring Watchboy to help him. Then he settled down, and worked as well as a more experienced dog all the way to London.

To take her mind off Bobtail, Becky began to ask William about London, and he had plenty to tell her.

"There's a lot of talk about war," he said, "and London is full of men of the trained bands. They say that Parliament wants to put the Earl of Essex in charge of them. He's on their side."

"Aren't any of them on the King's side?" asked Becky.

"Not many. One of the men let me look at his

musket. I held it and it was tremendously heavy. I nearly dropped it and all the men laughed at me. And all the apprentices are for Parliament. You should see them running through the streets and shouting against the Archbishop."

"Weren't you frightened?"

"No," said William. "It was exciting."

"Exciting indeed!" said their mother indignantly, as she moved about the table, clearing the plates away. "You should know better than to speak lightly of these matters. And you should have spoken up for the King."

"You have to be careful what you say in London these days," said Mr. Garson. "They are all for Parliament, and the King himself is away in Scotland, so some Scottish drovers told me."

"You always were one for holding your tongue for the sake of peace," replied his wife. "I'd tell them. I'd let them know whose side I was on."

"Things are bound to come to a head sooner or later," said Mr. Garson. "I very much doubt that we shall be taking cattle to London this time next year."

No more was said about the London news. Becky helped her mother wash the dishes, then she put on her warm cloak and joined William in the garden. The rain had stopped and a watery sun had broken through the clouds as they stood together looking out along the drove road which ran past the house. Flood waters in the low-lying fields surrounding the cottage turned silver and shimmered in the sunlight. Slender yellow leaves still clung to the willow trees that bordered the road and fluttered like tiny defiant banners.

"I hope he arrives soon," said William. "When the rain stops, there'll be frosts, and it might snow. We had snow last year in November, do you remember?"

Becky shivered and sighed, and raised her eyes to the distant Mendip Hills standing bare against the skyline.

William also looked towards Mendip, but in his mind's eye he saw the drove road going on, mile after mile, across the Wiltshire Downs, and still further to Hungerford and turning north at Newbury to join the Ridgeway at Isley. Then eastwards to the River Thames at Streatley and Goring, on to Maidenhead and Hounslow, through Paddington, and so into Smithfield. Standing there, William re-lived the journey both ways. Somewhere on that great length of road, he hoped Bobtail was making his way home.

3 : Bobtail sets out

Bobtail set off at a good pace and soon left Smithfield behind. He crossed the Fleet River, where he allowed himself five minutes to see what he could find among all the interesting household rubbish it carried. There was a good-sized bone, many days old, with some fine, strong-smelling pieces of meat still attached to it. He took it with him and trotted off through Holborn towards St. Giles's Fields. There, a big mangy dog took the bone from him before he had time to sample it. Bobtail fought half-heartedly to keep it, but he was in a hurry and the dog had a nasty look in its eye. The bone didn't seem worth the risk.

From St. Giles, his instinct led him to turn north and then west. He passed the grim gibbet at Tyburn, where two clattering corpses swung pathetically in the wind. This was where criminals were hanged, and their bodies were left on the gibbet as a warning to all other would-be law-breakers. Only honest people were allowed a decent Christian burial.

Bobtail left Tyburn and found himself in the country, heading towards Paddington. From now on, the going became difficult. The road was much muddier than it had been when he was going the other way, taking the cattle into London. Rags and tatters of cloud obscured the moon from time to time, and Bobtail trundled on through the black and white world with pale moonlight to help him on his way. More than anything else, he wanted food and then he wanted to sleep.

As he reached the outskirts of the village, the storm clouds blew up in earnest. The moon disappeared for good, and a heavy shower wetted the top layer of his coat. In no time at all, he was struggling through sticky mud and deep puddles as the rain turned the highway into a quagmire. He walked warily along the main street, keeping a careful look out for signs of food and a place to sleep. The rain pelted down, landing in hard droplets on his back, thudding into puddles and splashing back on itself. Parts of the road were awash with water, and Bobtail paddled through it up to his knees. As he thrust forward, his foot plunged into a hidden pothole and he tripped and fell in. He gulped down a mouthful of muddy water and had to swim two strokes before he could struggle out.

He gave himself an almighty shake that sent water arcing away from his body on all sides. The village might have been deserted. There was no sign of life in any of the cottages. All the inhabitants seemed to have decided to save their candles and their firewood and go to bed early. Bobtail walked right through the sleeping village and a mile beyond it. Then he sat down to scratch, and stopped, with his hind leg half way to his ear. He remained like that for almost a minute, the tiresome itch forgotten, and the hind leg immobile. He knew this place. He had been here before. The whole stretch of road was familiar. Last time he had walked along it, just before sunrise, he had been behind a herd of cattle, with William at his side.

He put his hind leg down. The flea that had troubled him had long since gone its way among the mats and tangles of his coat. Looking ahead, he could see the long, low building of an inn. A single light was shining bravely through the rain to encourage any travellers who were about that night. In the darkness beyond the lamplight, Bobtail could hear the uneasy movements of cattle and the yap of an impatient dog as it tried to settle its charges.

He walked towards the inn and heard the voices of a pair of drovers as they crossed the yard and went inside. This was the inn where the Garsons had stayed just over a week ago, and one of the maidservants had been a kind-hearted girl who had made a fuss of Bobtail and brought him a pan of water and some tasty scraps from the kitchen.

Bobtail trotted confidently through the archway and into the yard. He went straight to the kitchen door and began to scratch. No one heard him, but he could hear laughter and talking inside. He gave up scratching, and stood listening, head on one side and nose clapped to the bottom of the door. In less than a minute, it opened and before he could move aside the contents of a slop pail caught him full in the face. He yelped and ran towards the stable. This wasn't the sort of welcome he had expected. There was a scream from the kitchen and the door closed.

Safely inside the stable, Bobtail shook himself and then sniffed. The stuff which had fallen on him smelt good. He settled down in some straw and began to lick as much off his face as his tongue would reach. There was some on his chest too, which was easy to get at, and a lot on his legs and paws. While he was licking steadily, the door opened again and he heard cautious steps cross the yard. Then a girl's voice spoke.

"There *was* someone, I tell you. I heard them."

"Someone or something," said another. "It's a nasty old night. Come back in and we'll bar the door. There'll be no more guests tonight."

Bobtail leaped up joyfully. He rarely forgot a voice. The first speaker had been the friendly maidservant who had fed him the week before. He gave a short bark. There was a gasp and a running of steps back to the door and then a relieved voice.

"Oh, 'twas only one of the dogs."

The kitchen door closed, but Bobtail was determined to make it open again. He crossed the yard and began to scratch at it, digging his nails deep into the wood. He kept up a barrage of short, high-pitched yaps, quite unlike his usual deep bark.

"Drat the dog!"

The door opened suddenly and a broom was pushed into his face. Bobtail flinched, but stood his ground. He pushed past the girl, crossed the threshold into the kitchen, and stood there, shaggy and wet, with half an inch of bright pink tongue protruding from beneath his great black nose.

"Whatever in the world . . .?" It was the owner of the first voice. Bobtail moved over to her and sat down heavily. He lifted a dripping wet paw and placed it firmly against her apron.

"Get off, you dirty animal," she said crossly. "Look what you've done. I can't serve the gentlemen like this. We've gentry staying here tonight and we can't have the likes of you around."

She looked at her companion, who was turning a spit over the fire. "We'll have to get him out or there will be trouble."

She bent down towards Bobtail, who immediately rolled over on his back and waved all four paws in the air. He knew from experience that when he did that, it was almost impossible for anyone to get a proper grip on him.

"Well, just look at that!" said the girl, laughing. "We had a dog in here last week who did that. He was bigger, though, with a long fluffy coat."

Bobtail went on rolling, and the girl stepped closer. "I don't know but what this isn't the same dog. It could be, only he wasn't so wet then, you see, so I suppose he looked bigger."

Bobtail decided to risk standing up.

"It is the same," said the girl, "I'm sure it is. That one didn't have a tail and neither has he. And he's all wet, the poor thing."

Bobtail shook half a gallon of water out of his coat. The girl sprang back in dismay and her sympathy turned to scolding.

"You'll have to get rid of him, and quick," said the girl at the spit.

They found a piece of rope and tied it round Bobtail's neck. Between them, they dragged him, protesting, across the yard and shut him in the stable. Bobtail thought of jumping over the half door and trying to get back to the kitchen again, but the straw was dry and comfortable, and he lay down in it. A few minutes later, the girl brought him a large dish of scraps and a bucket of water, and he ate and drank happily. Then he turned round and round in his straw bed, scrabbled some of it closer round him, and flopped down with a grunt of satisfaction.

It was a restless horse that eventually woke him. Bobtail had dried out overnight and looked large and fluffy again. He stood up, yawned, stretched himself and shook most of the straw out of his coat. He had finished his water the previous night, so he drank from a half-empty horse bucket. Then he snuffed round in his bed and discovered a few pieces of meat he had dropped while eating his supper. He had been too sleepy to look for them at the time. Now they made him a good breakfast.

The sun had only just risen, but Bobtail felt the urge to move on. He gave himself one final shake, sat back on his haunches, took in the height of the door above him, measured his distance, and leaped over into the yard. Men and maids were already stirring, but his special friend was nowhere to be seen. He walked away from the inn and on to the high road.

4 : The stampede

Walking through a field, Bobtail surprised a ginger cat which had just caught and killed a rabbit. The cat ran off, alarmed at seeing such a huge, shaggy apparition as Bobtail, and the carcass of the rabbit changed owners.

People gave Bobtail water at the farms he passed, but finding a comfortable shelter for the night was quite another matter. Farm dogs were jealous of their territory and drove him off when he tried to make a bed for himself in a cow byre or outhouse. So he went back to the fields, and curled himself tightly between the huge roots of an oak tree.

That night there was a frost, whose nipping cold penetrated the still air beneath the hedge. Bobtail woke early to a tingling morning where each blade of grass was outlined with frosted dew, and a red sun ball was casting a rosy glow over the surrounding fields. But the day which had begun so dry and crisp clouded over as he moved west, and the frozen mud on the road melted to its usual stickiness. The countryside began to give way to a town, and Bobtail jogged towards it happily. Towns meant people and people meant food.

A market was in full swing. All the town's inhabitants seemed to be there, and many people from the outlying villages too. There would be no more markets until the following spring, so everyone was determined to make the most of this one.

Hunger drove Bobtail towards the livestock market, where he knew he would find food. But it was not easy to get near the shambles. The market was a seething hubbub of noise and movement. There was a goose fair next to the cattle market and the frenzied squawking of angry geese mingled with the cries of the butchers and the lowing of cattle. Bobtail had to get through groups of women who were picking their way through the dirty streets, their long skirts lifted an inch or so above the mud by the high-soled wooden pattens they wore on their feet. Men on horseback were pushing through the crowds of people on foot, and children were bowling hoops and playing tag among them all. At last Bobtail found what he wanted, and settled down to a meal of fresh meat.

While he was enjoying himself in the shambles, an enormous herd of fierce Dorset cattle, bound for London, was jostling its way right through the main street with its line of stalls. The animals were moving much too fast for anyone's safety, but there was little the drover in charge of them could do about it. His helper, a lad of about thirteen, had his hands full controlling fifty geese who were accompanying the cattle. They had one dog, but they needed at least two if the cattle were to be kept from doing serious damage.

The drover cursed the bad luck which had brought him to the town on market day instead of the day before, as he had planned. Cattle were always shod when they went on a journey, to prevent their hooves wearing down, but some of this herd had cast their shoes, and stopping to get them re-shod had taken twenty-four valuable hours.

The cattle took fright at the noise and bustle of the market. They started plunging at stalls, churning up the mud underfoot and fighting each other. To add to the confusion, a large, cumbersome coach, pulled by four horses, was coming towards them from the opposite direction.

When Bobtail heard the cries of the cattle, he left the livestock market and made his way back to the main street. The market-place was filled with frightened, rampaging beasts, bellowing their discomfort and trying madly to get away from the people who were surrounding them on all sides with sticks and staves. Instinctively Bobtail raced round to the back of the herd beside the drover, and joined in. He confronted the cattle which were trying to turn back and pushed them forward. He ran to the other dog and saw that it was more or less in control of one side of the herd, so he turned his attention to the other side. It was like working with Watchboy. He ran along beside them, trying to keep them within the confined space between the stalls. The oncoming coach got out of the way by overturning a stall and plunging down a side street. Now the way was clear for the herd. Bobtail and the drover's dog nudged unwilling legs and nipped tardy heels to keep the cattle moving through the town.

Bobtail had never met such wild cattle before, but he managed very well, until one steer turned on him and attacked him with its horns. He leaped away, but not soon enough, and the tip of one horn ripped into his side. But there was no time to stop; the other dog was still needing help, and the two of them brought the cattle together on some common land outside the town.

The dogs and the drover's lad rested with the geese and cattle while the drover returned to the town to make his peace with the people whose market day he had ruined. When he returned, he moved the cattle on, and Bobtail automatically took his place with the other dog. By evening, when it was time to stop for the night, Bobtail had put an extra five miles between himself and home. He was on his way back to London.

It was not until they stopped that he sensed that things were wrong. They had come to an inn which was unfamiliar to him. All his instincts urged him to get away and retrace his lost ground. But the inn offered warmth and shelter. He was tired, and his injured side ached, and the blood from the wound was stiff and clotted on his coat. While he stood, undecided between a cold, dark journey and the chance of food and rest, the drover came up to him.

"You're a good dog," he said gruffly. "I'm keeping you. I don't know whose you are, but I'm your master now, boy."

He tied a rope round Bobtail's neck and tethered him firmly to an iron ring in the stable.

Bobtail strained on the rope. He pulled backwards and tried to slip his head out, but the rope was too tight. He yelped and howled his protest against what had been done to him. Still the collar held. He danced on his hind legs and shook his head crazily from side to side, but the rope would not give. The drover's lad came into the stable to feed the dogs.

"Tush now," he said, giving Bobtail a friendly whack on his hindquarters. "You're a good one with the cattle, though you are a funny shape." He emptied a plate of scraps in front of the puppy. "Eat this and quieten down."

He fed the other dog and left both of them some water. Then he went back to the inn for his own supper.

Bobtail was still rebellious, but he ate because he was hungry, and then fell asleep, quite worn out by the day's adventure. He woke next morning feeling stiff. Hearing the familiar sound of cattle nearby, he thought for a moment that he was back with William and his father. But the pull of the rope on his neck as he stood up to shake reminded him where he was. Shaking was uncomfortable because of the pain in his side. His shoulder felt much stiffer than it had the previous night, and it hurt to put too much weight on his leg.

Getting away became a matter of great importance.

With his strong teeth, he began to bite into the rope. He bit and spat out pieces of hemp for half an hour before the final strand gave way. He was free. Only the lower half of the door was closed, and he scratched at it. It refused to move, so he leaned all his weight against it, but the latch held firm. So he squatted on his hind-quarters for a jump. The door must have been higher than he thought, or perhaps his injured shoulder spoiled his jump, for he failed to clear the top of it. He hit his front leg against the wood with a jolt that sent a terrible pain up through his shoulder, and fell back in a heap on the floor.

The drover shook his head when he found the chewed rope. He tied a fresh length on to the piece that was still round Bobtail's neck and led him, limping, out into the yard. The lad looked critically at the puppy.

"He's no good. He's limping after half a day's work."

"Nay, he's a good one, I tell you," retorted the drover. "Look how he got us out of that fix yesterday. He's lame because old Wall Eye gave him a biff with his horn. He'll have to learn how to be a bit more nippy on his feet, that's all. I must have two dogs with this lot if I'm to get them to London in good shape."

"He'll run away," said the lad, still looking doubtful.

"I'll see he doesn't get the chance," said the drover.

He made Bobtail walk up and down the yard until the stiffness eased a little in his swollen shoulder, and his limp grew less pronounced. Bobtail meant to escape the moment the drover let go of him to attend to the cattle, but he was given no chance. The drover fastened a rope collar to the other dog's neck, and tied Bobtail's rope to it, so that the two dogs should work roped together. This was sometimes done while training a puppy. But the older dog was not going to have a lame and unwilling partner attached to him. He turned on Bobtail and began to fight. He bit his ear and his face, and then his jaw sank into Bobtail's damaged side.

Bobtail fought back blindly, feeling that he was fighting not only for his freedom but for his life. The other dog was as fierce as the cattle he was in charge of. The two were tied together and neither could get far enough away from the other to launch himself at his assailant. Instead, they rolled over and over, lips curled back, strong teeth seeking any sort of hold. Bobtail felt himself weakening, but he fought on grimly.

He was dizzy and almost unconscious when the shock of cold water brought both dogs to a standstill. It was followed by yet another cold douche as a second bucketful came flying over them. Rough hands released Bobtail and a kick on the hindquarters sent him reeling away. He crawled beneath a hedge and lay panting and out of sight while the herd moved away. Then he limped down the field to where a stream was flowing through a small valley. Gratefully, he lowered himself to the ground and drank.

Then he heard footsteps running down the hill, and two boys appeared.

"There he is. That's the dog that was in the fight. He's hurt, I tell you."

"Keep away. He's a killer, that one."

A stone plopped into the water close to Bobtail's head. It was followed by several others. He stepped carefully into the stream and waded along it. The banks above him became steeper and steeper, and the dense growth of shrubs and brambles lining the banks closed over his head. They formed a tunnel through which he could pass, out of sight of the boys on the bank.

He scrambled out of the water further upstream, and lay panting on the grass. Then he began to shiver. It hurt to shake the water from his coat, although he really needed to get rid of it. He had been soaked to the skin by those buckets of icy water. He set off through the fields, dripping as he went, and for the rest of the day he avoided people as much as he could.

When dusk began to fall, he turned aside to enter a small hamlet, and crawled into a lean-to shed beside a cottage. The place was full of wood, neatly stacked, and a small chest stood on a carpenter's bench. Painfully, Bobtail settled down in the darkest corner on a pile of wood shavings and lay alternately burning and shivering until he managed to forget his troubles in an uneasy sleep.

5 : Bobtail finds friends

"Jack, look over there, in the corner."

"How did he get there?"

"He must have come in during the night."

Bobtail woke with a start. Two children were looking anxiously at him from the doorway. He sensed that they were friendly and tried to get up to meet them. But during the night, his shoulder had swollen and stiffened. He yelped as pain stabbed through his body.

"Oh, poor boy!" The little girl went to crouch on the floor beside him. She stretched out a hand, but Bobtail cowered away. He didn't want anyone to touch him.

"Come over here, Jack," she said. "He's badly hurt. On his shoulder and down his side."

Her brother looked at Bobtail, taking in the mud-stained, badly matted coat and the ugly wound which was obviously causing a lot of discomfort. He turned to his sister. "We'll get that shoulder looked at, but Father had better come to move him. Go and call him, Beth, while I make friends. He'll have to learn to trust us before we can help him."

While Beth ran to find her father, Jack remained beside Bobtail, drew a sack gently over him and spoke soothingly to reassure him. When the children's father arrived, he and Jack lifted Bobtail on to a wooden door which was standing against the wall, and used it as a stretcher to carry him into the house. Bobtail moaned a little as they moved him, but made no attempt to resist.

They placed him on sacks in front of the fire in the kitchen. With sympathetic murmurs, the children's mother fetched clean cloths and set two bowls on the

table. Into one she threw a handful of herbs which came from an earthenware jar on the floor beneath the window. Then she scooped hot water from a pot over the fire and poured some into both bowls. Leaving the herbs to infuse, she dipped a cloth into the other bowl. Very gently, she washed the dried mud from Bobtail's coat, and clipped the hair away from his shoulder with sheep-shears, leaving the skin exposed. Then she cleaned the wound thoroughly with the water in which the herbs had been soaked. Finally, she applied a poultice of herbs and strapped it firmly into place.

Afterwards, they fed Bobtail with broth and scraps of meat and gave him fresh water to drink. Then he eased himself into a comfortable position, and slept in front of the fire. Jack and his father went to the workshop to carve delicate flowers and scrolls around the lid of the chest, and the mother baked bread. Beth sat beside Bobtail nursing a doll and fondling his ears until they twitched in his sleep. Later in the day, her mother removed the poultice and put on a fresh one.

Bobtail stayed at the cottage with the carpenter's family while the herbs worked their magic on his shoulder. On the fourth day, the swelling went down, and the next day he could walk without limping. Then he was able to run and play with the children in the yard outside. He was feeling happier than he had been for a long time. But in the evenings he used to stand at the door of the cottage and sniff the air as it blew in from the west. On the evening of the sixth day, he put a paw over the threshold. The family watched him anxiously. Then he seemed to change his mind. He turned back to the fire and threw himself once more on his bed of sacks.

He was restless that night. The next morning, after a meal of oatmeal and water, he stood and looked at the family. He gave his bottom a little shake, as if to apologize for what he was going to do. He walked up to Beth's mother and licked her hand. He reached up to lick Beth's face as she bent down to stroke him. Then he turned his back on them and walked to the door. Beth's father rose, crossed the room and unlatched the door. He held it open for Bobtail, who walked out of the cottage and trotted purposefully down the road away from them.

Beth wept, and her mother found it hard to comfort her, because she missed the dog herself. Her husband consoled them both.

"He could never have stayed with us. He's a drover's dog, born and bred to herd cattle. He can't stay here and idle away his time now that he's fit and well."

"I'm glad we were here when he needed us," said his wife, and Beth knew there was no more to be said. But it was a long time before she stopped missing Bobtail.

Bobtail felt quite sure of his direction as he walked

down the road from the cottage. He covered many miles before darkness came, and hunger drove him to seek the shelter of an inn. He was making a cautious entry into the yard, when he heard his name called.

"Why, there's Bobtail!" A stout, jovial man appeared with a serving boy at his side. "Surely that's Bobtail. You remember. He came up a couple of weeks back with Garson's herd."

Bobtail was quick to sense a friend, and he recognized the place as one of the inns where he had stayed overnight with William and his father. He wagged his bottom, and jumped up and pawed the innkeeper in delighted recognition.

"Come on, old fellow, has your master left you then? You've been in the wars, I see." The innkeeper examined Bobtail's shoulder where the hair had been clipped off. "Well, someone's been taking care of you. Now let's see about a dish of something."

Bobtail had a large plate of scraps and a huge marrow bone for his supper that night. He lay in the straw and chewed and bit and sucked till his jaws ached. Finally, he fell into a dreamless sleep.

The next morning, after another good meal, he set off once more confidently in the direction of home, and made good progress until a pain in his foot made him stop. He sat down and explored the sore place with his tongue. It wasn't a stone. He was very clever at picking stones out of his feet. He licked and licked, but it only seemed to push whatever was hurting him further between his pads. William could have used his fingers to put it right, but there was no William, so Bobtail plodded on, limping to take the weight off his injured pad. Twice he stood in a stream which seemed to help. But the pain came back when he started to walk. At last he started running on three legs.

An hour later, he came across a cart which was

carrying a load of salt. It had stuck in a rut, and the carter was putting a plank of wood beneath the wheels and leading the horse forward by its bridle. When his cart was free, he threw the plank into the back of the cart and climbed on to his seat. As he took up the reins, he didn't notice the extra jolt as a large dog landed neatly among the sacks in the back of the cart. Bobtail stretched luxuriously between a couple of them. The jolting didn't worry him, and he licked busily at his paw until it felt better.

The cart rumbled on for mile after mile. The carter sang, and talked to his horse as it picked a difficult way through the hard-frozen countryside. As they passed through one village, church bells were ringing and groups of people, in their Sunday-best clothes, were making their way up the street to church. Some frowned to see the carter going about his business on a Sunday, but he was not a church-going man and travelled on any day that suited him. He stopped once, to rest his horse and have a meal, while Bobtail lay sleeping, undiscovered, among the sacks. Late that evening, they stopped outside an inn, and Bobtail sat up. The carter, who had come round to the back of his vehicle, looked at him with surprise.

"How long have you been here?" he asked. "Get out, dog!"

Bobtail jumped down and limped off towards the inn yard.

"Hurt your paw, have you?" said the carter, good humouredly. "Come here. Good boy."

Bobtail walked over and sat in front of him. He saw that a thorn had worked its way into the dog's foot, and soon had it out. Bobtail jumped up and licked his face.

"I can do without that," said the carter, pushing him off, but not unkindly.

He led his horse and cart into the inn yard and Bobtail followed. There was something familiar about the place.

"Hullo there." The innkeeper came out. "That's not your dog."

"No. He's a clever one, that. I've given him a free ride for I don't know how long. Never heard him get up. Knew what he was about, though. He had a thorn in his foot."

"That's Garson's pup," said the innkeeper. "They passed through here some time back. The dog's late. Something's held him up, I reckon."

"Funny-looking animal." The carter looked at Bobtail. "A bit comical. Attractive though. You don't see many of those about. The last one I saw was in Sussex, handling sheep. Making a good job of it too."

"It's a good thing you stopped here," remarked the

innkeeper, "or you would have taken him out of his way. Garson comes from Bridgwater."

While they talked, the carter unharnessed his horse and rubbed her down. Bobtail sat in the stall, waiting for the meal he was sure to get in this friendly place. The innkeeper leaned in the stable doorway and continued the conversation.

"Where are you taking your salt, these days?" he asked.

"I'm working for the army now."

"The army?"

"Yes. All army meat rations have to be stored in salt."

"But which army? Where?"

"Anybody's army." The carter laughed. "The whole countryside is full of armies. Men going off to join the Earl of Essex who's a Parliament man and in charge of the army in London. Men looking for the King to offer their services if there's going to be a war. King's men or Parliament's men, they all need salt."

"Whose side are you on?"

"It's no good taking sides in my job," said the carter. "Wherever I am, they stop me and I have to hand the stuff over. They're all armed, and I'm a peaceful man."

He turned to pick up a bucket of water for his horse, to find that Bobtail had been there before him. "Look at that," he laughed. "That dog's been licking more than his paw. I reckon he's licked the sacks and the sides of my cart. He'll be thirsty for twenty-four hours after that." Still laughing, he refilled the bucket and gave it to the horse.

Bobtail followed the two men into the inn, where he was given a generous helping of food and more water. The innkeeper was in such a good humour at seeing his friend the carter that he let Bobtail spend the night in the kitchen instead of sending him to the stable.

6 : A dismal Sunday

While Bobtail was travelling west with the carter, people down in Somerset were getting ready for church. Worshippers picked their way along the muddy drove road which ran past the Garsons' cottage. It was built on a causeway, so it stood above the flooded water meadows. All the same, the surface was bad. It had been churned up by the feet of hundreds of cattle which had passed along it during October on their way to market. The droving season was over now for another year. Robert Ashe, who owned Bobtail's mother and brother, had returned by coach three days after William and his father. Four days later, Robert Ashe's two dogs and the puppy had turned up, none the worse for their journey. Other dogs had been seen on their way home to West Country farms, looking tired and footsore. Their coats were plastered with mud, for the weather had not been kind to them. William and Becky knew all the droving dogs for miles around and checked them as they passed. Only Bobtail remained unaccounted for.

Mrs. Garson said she was tired of rubbing the landing window clean where the children's anxious breath and grubby fingers had clouded the thick glass panes. It was here that they waited for a view of Bobtail's shaggy figure to appear over the horizon. On that particular Sunday, Becky was sitting alone on the broad window-seat, with her head pressed against the glass. She had been there since dawn. She went down to breakfast and returned immediately afterwards to keep watch. Then she had to go away again to get ready for church. She hated going out in winter. On rainy days, when you went outside, you sank into mud over your ankles and were scolded for getting your shoes and dress dirty. On frosty days, you stepped uncomfortably on the top of frozen, rutted soil, and slipped and hurt yourself.

As she came back to the window, the bells changed their tune. The steady toll became an insistent clamour. Mrs. Garson called her final summons up the staircase, and Becky unwillingly left her post and ran downstairs. William was standing at the gate with his eyes fixed on the distant hills, oblivious of the rain. Becky knew what he was thinking.

"Stupid boy, look at you, getting wet through standing there," scolded his mother as she threw a sack over his head and shoulders.

"Bobtail will be wetter," said William gloomily.

Mr. Garson joined them and rested a hand on William's shoulder.

"It's a pity," he said. "Perhaps the pup was too young to be left alone. But you'll just have to get used to the idea. I doubt that we'll see him again. I've lost a good dog for the sake of getting that coach ride home. We should have walked back with him, just this once."

Becky cried all the way to church after that. William wished she would stop. He had to keep reminding himself that boys never cried, not even when they had lost their best friend.

The church was cold and dark enough to suit the children's mood. The Garsons walked up the aisle to take their places on the north side, underneath the pulpit. This had an ornately carved tester hanging above it, which acted as a grand sounding board for Parson Blickley's great rumbling voice when he preached his sermons.

Becky always sat by the wall beside her favourite

effigy of Lady Caroline Maybury, who had died twenty-one years before. Becky loved Lady Caroline, who lay there so peacefully in her pretty clothes with a ruff around her neck. Her head rested on an embroidered cushion with tassels at each corner. Of course, it was all carved in stone, but somehow the stonemason had managed to make her look real. Even the cushion looked soft. When Becky was bored, which she often was in church, she held imaginary conversations with Lady Caroline.

Today, as she turned towards the statue, she found herself looking at the little griffons that supported the embroidered cushion. Because they were dogs, they made her think of Bobtail, and she began to cry again. Her mother "tut-tutted" and people turned their heads to look at her, but it didn't make any difference. Parson

Blickley came into the chancel and they all stood up, but it was no good; Becky couldn't stop her tears. When the sermon began she looked down at her lap, afraid that the parson's eyes were on her because she was crying.

Parson Blickley climbed into the pulpit and announced that he had chosen two texts. The first one, he said, came from Matthew, Chapter Eighteen, verses twelve to fourteen. William sighed. Parson Blickley's sermons were too difficult for him to follow and far too long. He had often planned adventures for himself and Bobtail while they were going on, but since returning from Smithfield he had given up doing that. Parson Blickley opened the great Bible and his voice thundered through the church.

"'How think ye? if a man have a hundred sheep, and one of them be gone astray, doth he not leave the ninety and nine, and goeth into the mountains, and seeketh that which is gone astray.'"

William sat up. He found himself listening attentively to every word the parson was reading.

"'And if so be that he find it, verily I say unto you, he rejoiceth, more of that sheep than of the ninety and nine which went not astray.'" William looked at Becky, who was still crying and twisting her skirt between her fingers.

"'Even so it is not the will of your Father which is in heaven that one of these little ones should perish.'"

There was a pause for the congregation to think about the words. Then Parson Blickley announced his second text, taken from St. John, Chapter Ten. He turned the pages and found the place.

"'I am the Good Shepherd: the Good Shepherd giveth his life for the sheep.'" William did not understand the sermon which followed. The words of King James's Bible were simple, but when Parson Blickley explained them in his long involved sentences, William always lost the thread. Anyway, the texts had been enough for him. The Good Shepherd always looked after his sheep. If one were missing, he would leave all the others and go out and find it and bring it safely home, even if it meant danger to himself. William spoke to no one on the way home. He could not get those texts out of his mind.

The children were both very quiet for the rest of the day. Becky sat moodily at the window and stared over the grey flood waters until it was too dark to see any more.

That evening, Robert Ashe called to see their father. He had to take four cows to a farmer who lived in a village on the other side of Bridgwater the following day. His two sons were going with him and he asked if William would like to go as well. Normally, William would have been delighted, but this time he hesitated. Another plan had been taking shape in his mind.

"It's as you please," said Robert Ashe comfortably. "We shall be making an early start. If you feel like being a lazybones, you had better stay at home. Don't make up your mind now. But if you aren't there when we are ready to start, we shan't wait for you."

"I'm sure he'll come," said Mr. Garson. "He always enjoys an outing with you, Robert, don't you, William?"

William murmured non-committally, and soon afterwards Robert Ashe departed.

That night, William and Becky, lying in their truckle beds upstairs, found it difficult to go to sleep.

"You know, Parson Blickley was right," said William. His voice sounded muffled from the depths of the sheepskins he had pulled around himself for warmth.

"What do you mean?" asked Becky.

"About the shepherd going to look for the one that was lost, even though he had all those others."

"Ninety-nine," murmured Becky sleepily. As usual, when she started to talk, she found herself falling asleep.

"Yes. Ninety-nine. That's a lot. You'd think it was enough, but he wanted that other as well, because he loved them all and couldn't bear to think of anything happening to any one of them."

"He left everything and didn't stop looking until he had found it."

"Yes. Ninety-nine. Watchboy's the ninety-nine..." William's voice trailed off.

"What are you talking about?"

"Nothing," said William. "Go to sleep."

It was at that moment he saw how he could make use of Robert Ashe's invitation to suit his own purpose. It meant deceiving his family as well as Robert Ashe, but there was nothing he could do about that.

7 : Along the drove road

William woke with a start. He hadn't meant to fall asleep. Becky was breathing deeply and regularly as he slipped carefully out of bed. He put on his outer clothes, and went downstairs, carrying his shoes. Watchboy nearly gave him away as he entered the kitchen, but the growl died in his throat when he saw who it was. William put on his shoes and laced them. He took his thick cloak from the nail behind the door and wrapped it closely round himself. He found oatmeal in a jar in his mother's cupboard, and stuffed handfuls of it into his pocket. He pulled off a chunk of bread from a loaf on the shelf and helped himself to a couple of oatcakes. He took a knife, in case it should come in handy, and wondered about taking a length of rope, but decided that it would be too difficult to carry.

Moonlight seeped in through the tiny windows and showed him where things were, but the kitchen was so full of shadows that he had to move more slowly than usual. His stealthy preparations made Watchboy uneasy, and the dog began to whimper. William silenced him by cupping his muzzle firmly between his hand for a few seconds. Nell slept soundly, her paws and body twitching as she dreamed.

At last William decided he was ready to leave. He had to be well clear of the house by half past five, so that if anyone missed him, they would think that he had gone over to help Robert Ashe. He slipped the door bolts easily and went outside. As he pulled the door to after him, he heard the latch click loudly and held his breath. No one stirred in the house, and William heaved a sigh of relief. Then he set off with his face turned towards Mendip.

He stumbled awkwardly along the frozen, rutted road. The moonlight world was quite different from the daylight one. It was much more difficult to judge distances, and harder to pick out the smoothest places to walk. There were disturbing whisperings and rustlings too, as tiny wayside creatures scurried along paths known only to them. An owl startled William as it called from an ash tree above his head. A hundred yards away, another owl answered from the depths of the old oak which stood on a grassy knoll above the flood waters. William was not very happy. He was used to being out while it was dark, because all farm work began very early in the morning. But he always felt that he was in an unfriendly world which was never as safe as the daytime one.

Suddenly, his right foot went through the surface of a frozen puddle. Ice-cold water seeped into his shoe and invaded his foot. This was a bad beginning. He tried to wriggle his toes as he went along, to keep them warm, but he couldn't wriggle and walk at the same time. He gave it up as a bad job and pulled some oatmeal out of his pocket and ate it. Then he wished he hadn't, because he had meant to make his supplies last as long as possible and only eat when he was hungry.

He walked on, wondering when the sun would rise. He had no definite plan. He just wanted to be like the shepherd in the Bible story who went out to look for his sheep. Of course, it wasn't a sheep he was looking for, but the idea was the same. He felt sure that if Bobtail had managed to keep to the route they had taken on the outward journey, he ought to meet him somewhere along the way. At least he might hear some first-hand news of him. Just how he was going to convince grown-up people that he had every right to be wandering about the countryside alone, asking for news of a lost dog, he didn't know. He would manage somehow.

He went as quietly as he could through the first village he came to, afraid that watchful dogs might give him away. But they must have been asleep like their owners. He passed a dark cluster of buildings which he knew were byres where cattle sheltered on rainy days during the summer. He ate some more oatmeal. He wasn't hungry, but it was comforting and something to do. As he walked past the shapeless huddle of a farm standing close to the road, a dog barked. It must have been tied up, because it didn't come out to meet him. The farm was the last building on this stretch of road. Across the fields, he could pick out the denser black of buildings standing on high ground above the floods.

A sudden thought struck him. How long could he keep walking after daybreak without resting? And if he rested, perhaps Bobtail would pass him. When did Bobtail sleep? At night surely. He would be asleep now. He might this minute be sleeping in any one of the barns or outhouses that William had already passed. It was such a terrible thought that William stopped dead in his tracks. He might be going on and on in the wrong direction, all for nothing. Bobtail would arrive home later in the morning and William would be miles away.

He was so worried that he actually walked all the way back until he was in sight of his own home once more. At every deserted barn he passed, he called Bobtail's name. There was no response, except from one indignant householder who appeared at the window of a cottage and shook his fist at him. He stood in the road feeling stupid. His great idea had fallen flat. He had been up and down the same road twice. He had eaten too much of his small supply of food, and one foot was freezing cold. He wondered whether there was time to creep back indoors to find dry stockings and another handful of oatmeal. He even wondered whether to go back to bed.

As he hesitated outside the house, a glimmer of candle-light appeared in an upstairs window. It was probably his father, looking to see whether he had gone over to meet Robert Ashe. He turned and ran back along the road. He slowed down only when he was out of sight of the house, and after that he walked on steadily until he approached the outskirts of Glastonbury.

The hills in front of him stood black against a growing hint of dawn. He could see clearly now where the high land dropped steeply to the gorge at Cheddar. His eyes followed the hill-top westward along the ridge to the sharp outline of Crook Peak beyond Axbridge. From there, the land dropped gradually towards the sea. William had never seen the sea. One of his dreams had been to walk with Bobtail all along that ridge until he could look down on it. William shivered and hugged his cloak more tightly around himself.

He was tired now, and the road seemed unending. Then he rounded a bend and saw an inn. His tiredness was replaced by a great hope that Bobtail might be there. As he stood in the archway, a maidservant came out to the pump. William wondered what to say to her without arousing suspicion, but it was easier than he expected. The girl was half asleep, and she thought he was a serving lad, attached to some people who were staying there. She said that she had not seen Bobtail and added that there was ale in the kitchen if he wanted it.

William followed her and stood inside the door, looking around him. There was a delicious smell of baking and he saw a large batch of cakes on the table. The cook had been up before sunrise to make sure that there was enough food for the day's needs. Trying to look as if he had every right to be there, William moved over to the table and stretched out his hand towards the cakes.

A figure appeared in a doorway and William jumped back in alarm.

"Be off with you! I'll not have thieving boys in my kitchen!" A large woman was crossing the room towards him. She picked up a wooden paddle, used for beating the dirt out of clothes, and hit William across the shoulders with it. He ran out of the kitchen and across the yard. The little serving girl cried "Stop thief!" at the top of her voice. William expected to be overtaken and hauled back to explain himself. But no one bothered to take up the maid's cry, and he reached the safety of the fields. After that, he decided to avoid meeting people if he could.

As he left the fields and took to the road once more, he found that his eyes were closing. He had to sleep. There was a small barn about a hundred yards up the road. It was dry inside and there was a rough ladder leading up to a loft. William decided that it was safer to be above road level, and climbed into the loft without stopping to explore the ground floor. There was an opening in the upper chamber which overlooked the road. He lowered himself on to some hay and lay flat on his stomach with his face to the opening.

He woke two hours later to find the barn filled with light and shade, while outside the silver-frosted world of early morning had been transformed by cheerful winter sunshine. He climbed down the ladder and stood for a moment in the doorway, looking up and down the road. How long, he wondered, had he slept and had Bobtail passed by while he had been in the barn?

"Fine morning, lad," said a voice, and William gave a start.

"Ah, frightened you, did I?" An old man, dressed in filthy rags which had lost all likeness to clothes, with a tattered bundle beside him, was sitting in the shadows behind the door. "Had a good sleep?" he asked.

"Yes," said William. "How did you know I'd been asleep?"

"Guessed. Saw you climb the ladder."

"You weren't here when I came in," said William. "Nobody was. I looked."

"Didn't look far enough," said the old man. "I was right back. 'Twas too cold to be near the door."

"Do you live here?" asked William interestedly.

"Don't live nowheres," said the old man. His voice changed to a wheedling tone. "I don't suppose you have a little something to eat about you now?"

"I've some bread," said William. "It isn't much, but you can have some if you like." He felt in his pocket and passed over a piece.

"Thank you, lad," said the old man putting it into his bundle. "Now, you wouldn't have anything more about you, would you?"

"No I haven't," said William shortly. He didn't like the look in the man's eye and decided it was time to go. But first, there was a question to be asked. "If you've been here all the time, have you seen a big shaggy dog without a tail go by?"

The old man shook his head. "No, lad, I haven't," he said.

"You haven't been asleep, have you?" asked William.

"No. I have not been asleep," he answered. "I sleeps at night and just rests by day, when I'm not walking. Now, what's a fine lad like you doing out on his own?"

"I'm looking for my dog," said William and set off towards Glastonbury.

8 : Bobtail meets a giant

Bobtail left the inn on Monday morning, in company with his friend the carter. He jumped into the cart while the carter was harnessing the horse, settled himself comfortably among the sacks and waited for the cart to move.

"No you don't, boy!" The carter gave Bobtail a friendly whack. Bobtail wedged himself more firmly between the sacks.

"Look at that." The carter turned to the innkeeper, who had come out to see him off. "I'm not going your way. If you come with me, I'll take you to Bristol." He tried to take Bobtail by the scruff of his neck, but Bobtail twisted his head away and rolled over. He waved his feet in the air and it was impossible to move him.

The carter became impatient. "All right, you old grey bear. Come with me. You'll live to regret it."

He climbed into the cart, took up the reins, and waved goodbye to the innkeeper. As they passed through the gateway, Bobtail twisted on to his stomach. He lay with his nose on his paws, jolting in time to the cart.

They travelled for half the morning, and then the cart turned off the road and stopped in the grounds of a big house. Bobtail was bundled out of the cart, and an officer and a group of soldiers began to unload the sacks of salt. The carter took no notice of him. He didn't seem as friendly as before. When one of the soldiers threw a stone at Bobtail, he decided to make his escape. He went back to the road and sniffed the air. This was not the way home. He sniffed again and set off across the fields with his face towards the sun.

For the rest of the morning, he passed through fields and woods which were unfamiliar to him. He drank from streams, but didn't stop long enough anywhere to find food. He had to get back to familiar country. By midday, he reached a broad highway running from east to west. He was back on his road again. This was the way which led to William.

He soon left the road, because it was uncomfortable to walk on. The rutted surface was frozen so hard that the weak winter sun made no impression on it. He galloped through a field, scattering sparkling hoarfrost in all directions. A dark zig-zag blaze through the grass marked his progress. It was an untidy trail, the trail of a dog who was fit and happy and on his way home. He turned, headed off in another direction and charged towards the corner of the field, then swerved off at right angles and began to run round and round in wide circles. Then he threw himself down and rolled, rubbing his back this way and that over a strong-smelling chunk of grass where a fox had paused an hour before. He stood up and shook out his coat and made off again to a group of farm buildings.

All this exercise had sharpened Bobtail's appetite, and he approached the farmyard with interest. In a small byre two cows were tethered, and a pig lay asleep in a stye next door. Across a yard was the farmhouse, built with its front wall facing the road. This was where food would be, Bobtail decided. He crossed the yard and made for the farmhouse door.

He had almost reached the doorway when two large yellow dogs came at him from round the corner of the house, barking furiously. They threw themselves at Bobtail and bowled him over. The larger of the two dogs straddled him and gripped his throat. Its companion took one of his hind legs in its mouth and almost pulled it out of its socket. Bobtail writhed a little and then lay still. Couldn't they see he was on his back and offering no resistance? The dogs were not impressed by Bobtail's signs of peace, and the strong fangs sank further into his flesh. For Bobtail, being able to breathe suddenly became the most important thing in the world.

"Jester! Beau!" A powerful voice rang through the yard, and a huge countryman appeared and threw himself on the bigger yellow dog. The other dog took its teeth out of Bobtail's leg and slunk off. The man took the large dog by the scruff of its neck and forced it to let go of Bobtail's throat. It fawned and cringed at the man's feet, but he roughly pushed it aside and stooped to pick up Bobtail and carry him indoors. Bobtail did not trust the owner any more than his dogs. He struggled to get out of the imprisoning arms, but found that he was being held in a grip of iron.

When he was lowered on to the kitchen floor, Bobtail coughed, retched, spat and felt better. His leg was still sore, but he discovered that he could stand on it. A dish of water completed his cure. He wagged his bottom to express his gratitude and put up a paw to this kind giant who had turned out to be a friend after all. The kitchen darkened as two large shapes appeared to stand sheepishly in the doorway. The dogs had returned to see what was happening to the newcomer, but neither of them ventured to put a foot over the threshold.

Bobtail was enjoying himself now. He stretched his back legs and gave a shake to the damaged one to prove that it was better. Then he stretched his front legs, lowered his nose to his paws and left his bottom in the air. He looked up at the man through his shaggy hair. Then, with a sigh, he banged his backside on to the floor and relaxed, head on paws and eyes still on his rescuer.

"H'm," said the man. "There's little wrong with you, young fellow." His hands explored the body beneath the rough coat, now fearfully matted and muddy. "Ribs," muttered the man. "You must be hungry. If you were mine, I'd have the shears on you and all those mats would come off. Still, you aren't, and I'll leave you as I find you."

He turned away to a table, selected some scraps of meat and bread, and threw them in front of Bobtail, who ate them greedily. The two yellow dogs at the door growled softly, and Bobtail paused apprehensively.

"Go on. Eat," said the man. "They won't come in."

Reassured by the tone of his voice, Bobtail wolfed down the scraps and drank some more water.

"That's all." There was finality in the man's voice. "Now on your way."

He strode to the door and flicked his fingers at his own dogs, who followed him and allowed themselves to be chained to a post in the yard. The man returned to propel Bobtail from the house with a firm but kindly push from his boot.

"Off with you!" he said, and pointed to the road. The yellow dogs strained at their chains and leaped up and barked at Bobtail. The message was obvious, and Bobtail scurried through the gate and down the road.

Much later in the evening, on the outskirts of a tiny village, he caught a rabbit all by himself. He lay down beneath a sheltering bush and ate it with relish. Then he trotted on towards the houses, drank from a stream and turned off across some fields to a broken-down barn. He made his usual cautious entry, but it appeared to be empty. He was just scrabbling together some dirty straw which lay in a far corner when a large black cat startled him by leaping out of it. Its green eyes blazed and it hissed like twenty snakes. It scratched Bobtail's nose and shot out into the night. Bobtail recovered gradually from the shock and curled himself up on the straw. He fell asleep, nursing his nose between his paws.

9 : William in Glastonbury

It was cold in Glastonbury and the streets were almost deserted. A coach passed William and he looked enviously at the rich wool merchant who sat inside. The man was muffled in a huge fur coat. It made William's cloak seem very thin. However tightly he wrapped it round himself, the cold penetrated to his very bones. His mother always said that a meal warmed you up. He felt in an inside pocket for his two oatcakes. He was glad he hadn't given those to the beggarman.

There was nothing there. The pocket was empty. Worse. When he had set out from home, he had had some money in a purse. The purse had gone. It had contained a golden guinea, given him on his eighth birthday by an uncle. It represented a small fortune, and it was not to be spent until he was a man. The rest of his money was small change, which would have bought him a pie at a market stall. Losing this guinea was almost as bad as losing Bobtail. He would never dare tell his parents.

He wondered how he could have lost it. The inside pocket of his cloak was tied together with tapes, so that nothing could fall out. His mother had made it especially for him when he went to London. She said that pickpockets couldn't take anything from it so long as he tied the strings. And the strings had been tied. He had a special way of tying them. The uncle who had given him the guinea was a sailor and had taught him the knots.

William opened his cloak and examined a couple of tapes he hadn't yet undone. They were roughly knotted together. They weren't his knots. He bit his lip and clenched his fists as he remembered the beggar in the barn.

"That's how he knew I was asleep," he thought. "He didn't guess at all. He came up and picked my pocket while I was asleep. And he gave himself away by retying the knots wrongly. I hope somebody catches him and he gets locked up. I hate him."

He knew all about beggars, who were often hounded from parish to parish because no one wanted to be responsible for them. Every parish was supposed to look after its poor people who had no homes or money, but the parish constables often could not be bothered with them. If a beggar was found outside his own parish, he would be whipped or locked up. If he stole something in his own parish, he would be put in the stocks. If he stole something anywhere else, he could end up on the gallows.

William felt sorry for beggars, but he was afraid of them too. Many of them were wild men, looking hardly human. They went about half naked, wearing verminous rags. The old man he had shared the barn with that morning had seemed harmless enough. But he had stolen William's money while he was asleep.

William retied his tapes, using the proper knots, though he didn't know why he bothered, now that his pocket was empty. Glastonbury suddenly seemed a very unfriendly place. He walked glumly up the street, with his eyes on the ground. Suddenly he heard a warning shout, but it came too late and he tripped over a hoop which had been bowling down the hill towards him. He picked himself up and returned the hoop to its owner, who examined it for damage.

"Look where you're going with that hoop," said William.

"Look where you're going yourself," said the hoop's owner.

He was a boy of William's own age, and the two stood and glared at each other. The three other younger children who shared the hoop also glared. William thought it was time to change the subject.

"Have you seen a big shaggy dog without a tail?" he asked. The children looked at each other and shook their heads.

"Why?" asked the boy with the hoop.

"Because I've lost him," said William.

The children turned their backs and sat down at the roadside with the hoop at their feet. The eldest opened a brown handkerchief bundle and produced four pies. There were three small ones and a big one. He gave a small pie to each of the three children and kept the big one for himself. He held it up and took an enormous bite out of the side.

"Can I have a bit of that?" asked William.

"Why?"

"I'm hungry."

"Go and buy one. There's a woman who sells them."

"Our mother made these," said one of the children.

"I haven't any money," said William.

The boy shrugged his shoulders and took another bite.

"Please!"

"What'll you give me?"

"I haven't anything. A beggar stole all my money, and my oatcakes."

The boy went on chewing.

"I've got a knife," said William desperately.

The boy stretched out a hand. Reluctantly, William took his knife out of his belt and gave it to him. It was a lovely knife, the kind grown-ups used. His father had bought it for him while they had been in London. Bobtail had been with them at the time.

The boy stood up and, at a sign from him, the others stood up too. He broke off a very small portion of his pie and offered it to William.

"That's not enough in exchange for a knife," said William.

The boy threw the piece of pie on the ground at William's feet and ran off, followed by the others.

William ran after them, but they suddenly turned into a house and slammed the door in his face. He walked slowly back and picked the pie out of the gutter. He wiped the mud off and ate it. It tasted good, but it was not worth the loss of his knife.

Outside the town, he took the road to Wells. He called at three inns along the way and asked the servants for news of Bobtail. At each place, the answer was the same. Nobody had seen the dog. The pie had made him thirsty, and he stopped to scoop water from a brook. He was down on his knees, drinking from his cupped hands, when he realized he was not alone. He looked up to see the brown face and grimy features of the beggar leering down at him. He jumped up and faced him.

"What do you mean, creeping up on me like that?"

"I wasn't creeping. I just walked."

"How did you get here anyway? I left you at the barn miles back."

"I passed you in the street. You was playing with some children and a hoop."

"I wasn't playing," said William angrily. He thought of the knife he had lost, all because his money had been stolen. "You came up into the loft while I was asleep," he said accusingly.

The beggar's eyes opened very wide. William noticed how blue they were in the brown, wrinkled face.

"Me? Up in the loft! I can't climb ladders, boy."

They were walking along the road together and the beggar began to put on a limp.

"I bet you can," said William. "You can climb ladders and you can take other people's belongings."

"Oh, young sir," said the beggar, "do I look that kind of person?"

"Yes," said William.

He tried to walk faster, but the beggar kept up with him. William could hear his wheezy breath just behind his left ear.

"I do wish you'd leave me alone," he said.

"Now why would you want to be left alone, young master? Running away, are you?"

"Of course not," said William sharply, "I'm looking for my dog. I told you."

"It's my belief you're running away," said the beggar. He caught up with William and placed a hand on his shoulder. William tried to shrug it off, but the hand stayed there.

"You and me. We'd make a good pair. We'd look after each other. I'd show you where to sleep at night and I'd teach you to snare a coney and take a goose from a rich man's garden."

"I don't need your help," said William. "And they can hang a man for stealing poultry."

"Not if you're clever they won't."

"You don't need to steal, anyway," said William bitterly. "You've got my money."

"Have I now?" said the beggar. He chuckled in his throat and William felt afraid. The beggar took William's arm. "Give me a helping hand, lad. I'm not as young as I was."

They walked along together for a quarter of a mile without speaking. The beggar's body smelt, and his breath was foul. William was planning how to get rid of him when they heard shouts from a flooded field below them.

Two men, waist-deep in water, were trying to bring a couple of half-drowned ewes to the bank. William saw his chance.

"Come on," he said, "do a bit of work for a change."

"Not me, lad, I'm no farmer's boy."

"Well, I am," said William, and scrambled across the

ditch, and lowered himself into the water.

The creatures were in a bad way by the time they had been carefully floated to dry land. William raced to the farm and brought more men, who came with planks. The ewes were lashed to them and carried into the byre.

The farmer told William to come to the farm to have his clothes dried, and gave him a meal. His wife, who might have asked awkward questions, was staying with her sister, and the men believed William when he said he was on his way to visit an uncle in Wells. He put on his clothes and set out.

He looked carefully up and down the road. The beggar seemed to have gone. William was glad to be rid of him. He started up the road, and then remembered something. He ran back to the farm, but no one there had seen Bobtail.

10 : The Wise Woman

As he walked along, William wondered where he was going to spend the night. In the distance, he could see the twin towers of Wells Cathedral. If he got that far, he might sleep in the shelter of its walls. He kept an eye open for the beggar. Wherever he slept, he was not going to share a roof with him.

It seemed to be getting dark earlier than usual. He would not reach Wells by daylight, and he wanted to be off the road as soon as it was dark. A few houses, dimly seen through the gloom, told him that he was coming to a small village. He wondered whether the beggar had stopped there. It might be just his bad luck to meet him again.

He thought about the Good Shepherd. He didn't feel very much like him at the moment. It made all the difference if you were grown up. He was sure the shepherd in the Bible story was a man. But he wanted to find his dog as much as the shepherd had wanted to find his sheep. Shepherds in the Bible were troubled by wolves. He seemed to be troubled by a beggar, who was a sort of wolf, frightening and dangerous. William remembered that Parson Blickley had said Jesus was the Good Shepherd who looked after people. He decided to ask the Good Shepherd to look after him.

He knelt down at the side of the road. He supposed he could pray standing up, but it seemed better to kneel, somehow.

"Please God," he prayed, "send the Good Shepherd to look after me. Don't let anything bad happen to Bobtail. Let me find him. Bless me, and Father and Mother and Becky, and don't let them worry. Amen."

He stood up and walked on towards the group of houses ahead of him. He went slowly past them, looking anxiously at each house, wondering what he should do. Houses meant people and people meant questions. A barn or cow-shed would be safer, if it were not for the beggar. It was a very small village, and William walked right through it before he had made up his mind. The road beyond the village ran through a wood, and he didn't like the idea of woods at night-time.

Just beyond the last house there was a tumbledown barn. He looked at it. That was just the sort of place the beggar would use. He could almost hear him saying: I'll show you where to sleep at night. "No you won't," said William to himself, and he turned away.

Just then, a black cat shot under his feet and ran across the road. He watched it run up to a cottage which stood some way from its neighbours. It could hardly be called a cottage; it was just a tiny hut with mud walls and reeds laid on branches for its roof. There was one little unglazed window in the wall through which smoke was escaping, and more smoke curled from a hole in the roof.

As William stood looking, a woman came to the door and lifted the cat into her arms. She walked down the path towards him, carrying the cat. She came so close that William could hear it purring. The woman looked very poor, but not at all rough. She was young and slender and had long fair hair. The hut behind her looked homely and the light in the doorway was welcoming. William took two or three hesitant steps forward.

The woman turned back towards the cottage. William had no idea whether she had seen him or not.

He ran up the path towards her, and she paused in the doorway, while the great black cat turned its green eyes towards him. She put the cat down and smiled. She held out a hand.

"You're cold," she said. "Come in and warm yourself."

She led him into her home, which was one tiny room with a beaten mud floor. In the centre of the floor, a bonfire was burning, giving both heat and light. A goat was tethered in one corner, and in another was a pile of bedding and a rough wooden table. William found it difficult to see very much until his eyes had grown accustomed to the dim light and the smoke. Then he began to see other interesting things. There were bundles of herbs hanging from the roof. One corner of the floor was littered with baskets of all shapes and sizes. In another there were jars filled with powders and coloured liquids, all carefully labelled. And there was a big wooden chest, covered with curious carvings.

William sat on the floor and turned his face to the fire. He stuck his cold feet towards the blaze and held out his chilled hands. The cat sat beside him with its eyes fixed unblinkingly on the flames, and ignored him.

"You'll be hungry," said the woman, and brought him oatcakes and goat's milk.

While William ate, she sat on the far side of the fire. William could hardly see her through the flames. He could just make out that she was spinning goat's wool.

Half-way through the meal, William yawned. The hot fire was making him sleepy. He told himself that he must keep awake while he made up a good story to explain where he was going. The woman was sure to ask.

She left her spinning, and William braced himself for her questions. He still hadn't thought of a good story. She surprised him by saying, "You're tired," and asking no questions at all. Instead, she arranged some sacking

and goatskins against a wall. She led William to them, and said simply, "Go to sleep."

William settled himself on the sacks and pulled the goatskins round him. He lay there for some time, watching the firelight flickering over the walls, sending crazy shadows of the cat and the woman dancing all over the cottage.

He began to notice other shadows. There was the goat, and that other one was the tall jar with the narrow neck which stood beside the carved chest. William watched dreamily. Then another shadow leaped up beside him. It looked like an owl with long ears. And there was another of a creature with a bushy tail. William looked over towards the woman. She seemed to have noticed nothing. She was still spinning. The cat continued to sit by the fire, and the goat stood patiently in its corner. William decided he must have been imagining things. His eyes followed the smoke drifting lazily up from the fire. It was all very peaceful. He wondered what Bobtail was doing at this moment. Suddenly he stiffened.

Out of the whirling smoke, close to the roof, a pair of round eyes stared down at him. Round eyes in a round head topped by narrow ears. Was he going crazy? A rustle came from somewhere above his head; a squirrel was perched on one of the branches that formed part of the roof, eating a nut. It was real enough. It was throwing the shells down on to his bed, and it had a splint on its hind leg.

He heard a soft cooing noise and saw a pair of collared doves on a perch beneath the roof. One of them seemed to have a broken wing. As his eyes travelled round the room, he saw many more woodland creatures. A pair of field-mice swung in a cradle made from an old stocking, and a jackdaw, with its wing carefully bandaged, cocked a beady eye at him from a perch over the door. More birds roosted in the branches above him.

William could hardly believe his eyes. He looked along the floor. All those baskets were really cages. There was a stoat with a bandaged paw in one of them, and a badger with a nasty gash on his shoulder slept in the largest. When a quivering heap of shining black fur on the floor turned out to be an otter, William sat up.

"Where have they all come from?" he asked. "Who *are* you?"

The woman looked up from her spinning and smiled.

"They call me the Wise Woman," she said. "Although there are some who give me an unkinder name."

"But the animals?"

"I am a healer," she said. "The people in the village come to me when they are ill, and the animals come too."

"You must be very clever," William said.

The woman laughed softly. "Go to sleep," she said.

And William did.

The next morning he woke feeling stiff, for the floor was hard. He stretched himself and lay looking around the room. The owl was asleep; the badger was up and scratching himself. The squirrel was eating more nuts and dropping the shells on to William's face. Some of the birds were down on the floor eating oatmeal. Over in the corner, the woman was milking the goat. The cat and the otter had disappeared.

"Where is the otter?" asked William.

"In the stream," said the woman. "Get up and have your breakfast." She gave him warm milk and put a wooden platter with bread and goat's cheese on the floor beside him.

William ate and drank obediently and watched her as she stirred a cauldron which hung over the fire. Except for the crackle of burning wood and the hiss as rain fell through the hole in the roof on to the fire, there was silence in the hut.

"You never asked me what I was doing, out at night," said William.

"I knew you would tell me if you wanted to."

"I'm looking for my dog. He's a puppy. But he's so big and shaggy that you'd think he was older."

"I haven't seen him," said the woman, "but I think he is near."

"Why do you say that?"

"I don't know why I say it. But that is what I feel."

"Am I going to find him? Can you tell me that?"

The woman didn't answer. Instead, she went to the

wooden chest and lifted the lid. She searched among its contents, and when at last she drew out her hand, she was holding something which glistened and shone in the firelight. William saw that it was a purple stone, curiously carved, hanging from a chain. She put it round William's neck.

"It's an amulet," she said. "Wear it as a talisman. It will bring you and your dog together, although I cannot tell you when."

"Thank you," said William. "Oh, thank you."

"Now," said the woman, "go and find your dog."

William waved to her from the road. Then he set off into the rain, taking the road to Wells and fingering the amulet which hung beneath his cloak.

It was Tuesday, he remembered, and he had been away from home for more than a day. He tried not to think about his family, and to concentrate only on Bobtail.

On that same Tuesday morning, Bobtail sat up in his barn, yawned, scratched himself, stood up to shake and sat down again to have a second scratch. He felt like another nap, so he turned round ten times, stirred up the straw with his foot and curled himself into a tight ball. Two minutes later, he sat up in alarm as a black cat ran through the doorway and pounced on something which squeaked in the straw. Bobtail recognized the black cat. It emerged from the tussle with a rat hanging limply in its mouth, and ran out into the rain. Now that he had been disturbed, Bobtail was thoroughly awake and ready to move off. He stood outside, sniffed the air, and set off towards home.

11 : News at last

Bobtail was looking for food. There were no rabbits in the fields, so he stopped at a house. It was quite a grand one, with a well-kept garden. Bushes and trees grew close to its walls, and Bobtail trotted up the path and lay beneath a holly bush. He chose the holly bush because it was growing beside a door. The door was closed. Bobtail lay on the dead, prickly leaves and watched it. He was used to closed doors. If he waited long enough, they always opened in the end.

At last his patience was rewarded. A young kitchen maid with a sack over her head to keep the rain off ran out to pick some cooking herbs from the garden. She had left the door ajar, so Bobtail whipped round it and into the big kitchen. The room was empty, except for a cat which dozed in front of the fire. The fireplace was huge and kettles and cauldrons hung suspended from hooks in the chimney. On the kitchen table, a joint of meat, prepared for the spit, was lying on a wooden plate.

Bobtail jumped up, seized the meat in his large jaws, and ran off with it, almost colliding with the maid in the doorway. Her shrieks brought other people to the scene. They flung stones at Bobtail, and someone chased after him. The meat flopped about in his jaws, and he stopped to arrange it more firmly in his mouth. The person who was chasing him almost caught him then. But Bobtail was off again and soon left his pursuer far behind. He found a narrow path leading up into the hillside above the house. He ran up it and carried his prize into a small wood where he could eat it undisturbed.

It made a wonderful meal, and Bobtail ate far too much. It was dry beneath the trees and, with a full stomach, he slept for hours. When he woke, he chewed some more meat from the bone. Then he walked out of the wood and down the path to the road, taking his bone with him. He ambled along at a steady pace, stopping several times to drink. The meat had been very salty and it made him thirsty. He walked through Glastonbury with the bone still in his mouth, and met no dogs to challenge him for it.

He reached a village a few miles outside the town just as a storm was breaking. Lightning flickered and thunder crashed as he ran through the pelting rain to look for shelter. He found it at last in a stable beside a house. Inside, there were two stalls but no horses, and he made himself comfortable in the one further from the door. After some tremendous shaking, he lay down and gave his full attention to his bone. About half an hour later he stood up and drank deeply from a bucket in the corner. Then he went back to his straw, turned round a few times and settled himself to sleep, with his bone carefully hidden beneath him.

He was wakened later when a horse was led into the empty stall beside him. It was dark, and the man worked by the light of a lantern as he rubbed his horse down, fed and watered it. Bobtail lay quietly and at last the stable door was closed and bolted. He and the horse were left alone for the night. He wriggled into a comfortable position and slept happily. He had no idea that he was locked in.

"What's happened to the sun?" thought William miserably, as he crossed the open space in front of the great West doors of Wells Cathedral. The wind was driving rain on to his back. His cloak was wet through, and he felt damp across the shoulders. This was the second time he had been in Wells that day. He reached the city for the first time about half an hour after leaving the Wise Woman's house, but a pedlar in the market place told him that he had seen a dog like Bobtail at a farm in Priddy the day before. Priddy lay several miles off the drovers' road, high up in the Mendip Hills. William spent the rest of the morning walking around in the mist and rain, calling at farms in the bleak countryside and asking about Bobtail. He had drawn a blank everywhere he went. Unless a farmer was hiding him, Bobtail was not in Priddy.

Now William was back in Wells, taking a short cut to the drove road. He passed from the cathedral into Penniless Porch, where the beggars gathered, and looked warily at them, to see if the one he knew had joined them. Then he came out into the market place. A little knot of men was standing beneath the archway which led to the Bishop's Palace. William was curious and hung about the edge of the crowd. Had somebody found a stray dog? He slipped between two stout men and came face to face with the beggar.

Two parish constables had him by the arms. Beneath the grime and the tan, the man's face was grey with fear.

"What's happened?" whispered William to a man standing in the crowd.

"He's stolen a goose from the Bishop. He's going to hang for it."

The beggar pointed at William, shaking one arm free from the constable's grip.

"The young master! He knows me. He'll tell you I never did it. I was with him yesterday."

William found everyone looking at him. One of the constables fixed him with a stern eye.

"This man is charged with stealing a goose yesterday

afternoon. Were you with him yesterday?"

"Yes," said William.

The second constable nodded his head knowingly. "Ah," he said. "So you were both together, were you?" He left the beggar and took William's arm. "You both stole the goose."

"Of course I didn't," said William crossly. "We didn't," he corrected himself, as he watched a bead of sweat run down the beggar's face into his beard.

"Then what were you doing?"

"We were outside Glastonbury. We helped a farmer get some ewes out of the flood. It took all afternoon."

"Was he with you?"

"Yes," lied William.

"Who are you?"

"I'm William Garson."

"Where do you come from?"

"Bridgwater."

"What are you doing here?"

"I'm here to collect one of my father's dogs."

"A likely story."

William swallowed hard. The man didn't believe him and he was going to share the beggar's punishment because he had said that he knew him. Help came unexpectedly. A man who looked like a drover spoke up.

"I reckon the lad's telling the truth. I know John Garson from Bridgwater."

William turned eagerly to him. "You know my father?"

"Yes, lad. We all know Jack Garson. One of the best drovers in the West Country. We've taken our herds to Smithfield together many a time." The drover looked solid and respectable, and the constables were inclined to believe him.

"So he helped you rescue some ewes when he was supposed to be stealing a goose?"

"Yes," said William. He told them exactly what had happened when he helped with the sheep, but pretended that the beggar had been there too. The crowd, which had been against the beggar, changed its mind after William had spoken. Reluctantly, the constables had to let their prisoner go. They hadn't actually found him with the goose, so he was let off with a caution.

"If we find you in this parish after sunrise, it's the gallows for you. We've heard tales about you. Snaring deer in Mendip Forest, some say. That's treason."

The beggar shuffled away and William hurried in the opposite direction before anyone could stop him. He wanted to avoid meeting the drover who knew his father. When the crowd had gone, he retraced his steps and made for the drove road. A figure slid out from between two houses. It was the beggar.

"Go away," said William.

"You did me a good turn back there, lad. Now, if we stuck together—"

"I've told lies for you, isn't that enough?" said William. "You've got to be out of here before nightfall. Why don't you go?"

"Come along with me," wheedled the beggar. "I need a strong lad like you to help me."

"No," said William. "I'm not coming. I'm going in the opposite direction and I don't ever want to see you again. Next time, you can hang."

William walked out of Wells, glad to see the last of it. He had wasted a whole day and now it was growing dark. He walked towards the lights of a farmhouse beside the road. He was hungry, but if he went to the house the people there would ask questions. It would be better to sleep in one of the barns beside the house. At least the beggar wouldn't be there.

He began to climb the gate, and was sitting astride it when two yellow dogs rushed up and began to bark at him. William sprang back into the road as their owner appeared. He was an enormously tall man and he looked at William suspiciously.

"What do you want?" he growled. "We don't encourage young thieves and vagabonds. Be off."

"I wasn't thinking of stealing anything," said William and he turned on his heel and set off along the road.

The giant obviously had second thoughts, because he called William back.

"What do you want?" he asked again, but more kindly this time. "It's a bad night to be out alone. Come in and get dry. Unless you've a home in the village, which I doubt."

William hesitated, but the man was holding the gate open for him.

"I'm looking for my dog," he said as he came into the yard. "He's a grey bobtail and he's overdue from Smithfield."

"Ho, are you?" said the man. "Then you're heading in the wrong direction. He was here yesterday morning and he went off the way you've just come."

"*What!*" William swung round and made for the gate.

"Now don't do anything in a hurry." The man put his hand firmly on William's shoulder and steered him towards the house. The two yellow dogs fell in behind. "You're soaked through and I'm sure you're hungry. Boys always are."

"But I must go after him," insisted William.

"Why?" asked the man. "The dog's all right. He can take care of himself, which is more than you can, by the look of you."

He took William into the same kitchen where Bobtail had been fed the day before. The man took a lamp and shone it into William's face.

"You're very young," he said. "I doubt if your parents know you're out here. Come on, here's food. You can eat up and tell me all about it. But perhaps we'd better get those wet clothes off first."

William sat by the fire, wrapped in rugs, while his clothes dried. He drank good, warming stew and ate satisfying chunks of fresh bread. He told his story and the man listened without speaking until he had done.

"The Good Shepherd?" He laughed. "Well, I like a

lad who cares so much for his dog. I had a boy like you once. He died, and his mother too. A sailor home from Bridgwater called at the house and brought the plague with him."

He stopped speaking, and looked into the fire for a time and William said nothing. Then the man roused himself and looked up.

"Your father was right. A good dog will find his way home. You and he should have had more faith in that Bobtail of yours."

William agreed and yawned.

"You had best put up on a couple of skins for the night," said his host.

"I ought to get back," said William. "It's not only Bobtail. It's my family too."

"It's too far to get there tonight," said the man practically. "Tomorrow, my brother is going to Glastonbury. He goes every Wednesday. I'll put you up on the saddle behind him."

William had to be content with that. He knew that sleep was all he wanted now. His head nodded and jerked lower and lower towards the table, and he fell asleep with his head on one arm, still clutching a piece of bread. He was still fast asleep when the man picked him up and took him upstairs, and he slept soundly until morning.

12 : Locked in

Bobtail sat up in his stall. It was still dark inside the stable, but sunlight was streaming in from a tiny barred window above his head, making a warm, sunny patch where he was lying. He nibbled at a flea, then lay back, warm and comfortable in the sun's bright rays. He stretched out a back leg and sent his bone scudding across the floor. It thudded against the partition, and the horse in the next stall snorted nervously.

Bobtail fetched his bone and took it back into the sunlight. For half an hour, he sucked at it, drawing out the sweet tasty marrow from the inside. Then he wanted a drink, so he went over to his bucket. This was almost empty and he visited the horse next door. The horse looked at Bobtail and stretched his face towards him. They rubbed noses and then the horse lifted its head and shook its mane.

It was time to go, and Bobtail turned towards the door. He lifted a paw and pushed, but the door remained shut. So he stood on his hind legs and put all his weight behind his next effort. It gave about half an inch as the bolt moved in its catch. He sat down and began to scratch at it. He scratched so hard that he left deep score marks on the wood. The door shook and rattled, but it would not open. Bobtail set up a series of frustrated yelps and angry barking. Still no one came.

The owner of the stable sat inside his house, bent over a scientific book. He had ridden into Glastonbury the day before to buy it, sat up most of the night reading it by candlelight, and had risen the next morning as soon as it was light in order to finish it. He

was a scientist, and when he was reading, or working at one of his experiments, he could think of nothing else. So he never noticed the row that Bobtail was making.

For three solid hours, Bobtail barked and fretted and howled. All over the village, people looked at each other, and wondered what could be happening to make a dog behave in such a fashion. They shook their heads and told each other that the mad man in the house on the edge of the village was raising spirits.

For three hours, the man read his book and made notes. Then, with a sigh, he closed it and sat back. He rose from his stool and flexed his stiff fingers. He glanced out of the window. It was raining again, and what was making that racket in his stable? He took a cloak and threw it round his shoulders, opened the door, and flinched as rain dripped from the thatch and found its way down his neck. Big drops fell heavily on the beaten mud of the yard and bounced back again as he skirted the puddles and made his way to the stable.

A dog was howling and the noise grew louder as his footsteps sounded across the yard. He hesitated. He wasn't very fond of dogs. How on earth had one come to be shut in his stable? He went back to the house and returned with a stout oak cudgel in his hand.

A huge, bear-like creature rushed out at him the moment the door was opened. He had no chance to use the cudgel; Bobtail leaped up to lick his face by way of thanks and knocked him on to his back in a puddle. Painfully he picked himself up and was immediately knocked down again as Bobtail returned to fetch his bone from the stable. He trampled all over the man as he ran out with it in his mouth and dashed through the gateway. He was a hundred yards down the road before his rescuer had collected his wits and risen to stagger back to the house.

William woke slowly to a cold, sunny morning, and found himself lying in a welter of animal skins on a narrow bed. He looked up at the rafters, where a huddle of downy sparrows were gathered in a sleepy bunch against the warm chimney-breast. For a moment, he thought he was in the Wise Woman's house. Then he heard the barking of dogs, and a deep voice calling to them, and he remembered where he was. He tumbled out of bed with a rush, put on his shoes and stockings and smoothed the creases out of his clothes. He picked up his cloak and went downstairs.

His friend of the previous evening was bending over a fire, stirring a pan of oatmeal and watching a pan of milk which was warming beside it.

"Good morning," he said to William.

"How soon shall we be leaving for Glastonbury?" asked William.

The man laughed. "Soon enough," he said. "But eat and drink first. You must keep up your strength and it will help pass the time before my brother comes."

"Will he come early?"

"He will come when he is ready. Now, do me the favour of eating the breakfast I have prepared for you."

William ate his breakfast, and afterwards the farmer gave him some oatcakes for the journey. He was just putting them in his pocket when a man on horseback appeared in the yard.

"Here is James," said the farmer, going to the door. "He doesn't know about you, of course. But he always calls here to see if I have any errands or messages."

It was soon settled, and William was hoisted on to the broad back of the horse behind James, who was every bit as large as his brother. With a final wave and a lot of barking from the dogs, they left the farm. William clung to James's belt, and settled himself to the rhythm of the horse as they set out for Glastonbury. The animal moved slowly, and William wanted James to whip it up, but didn't dare suggest it. They reached the town at last, and William said goodbye outside the church of St. John. It *would* start to rain, he thought, holding his hood tightly over his head. Angrily, he moved aside as a passing coach lurched by, splashing his face with mud when one of its wheels dipped into a puddle as it came abreast of him. His fingers closed around the amulet which still hung about his neck. If it really was going to help him find Bobtail, it would have to work pretty quickly. He was almost home.

He asked passers-by about his dog, with little hope of success. Some people thought they had seen him, and then contradicted themselves and said they hadn't. William walked down to St. Benedict's church at the lower end of the town. The rain was falling faster and he almost decided to shelter in the porch, but the thought that there might still be time to catch up with Bobtail made him decide against it. He turned quickly away from the building, and collided with a man coming out of a bookshop, carrying several volumes tied together with a leather thong. They flew out of his hand and the man cried out in alarm as they fell towards the gutter. William stooped and caught them neatly before they landed on the ground.

"Well done!" exclaimed the man. "I should indeed be sorry to see those fall into the mud."

He unloosed a horse which was tethered to a ring in the wall. "I really am most grateful," he said as he prepared to mount. Then he seemed to notice how young William was. "Are you all alone?" he asked. "Is there anything I can do for you?"

"Yes, there is," said William. "Could you give me a lift? I live along the road to Bridgwater. Only would you mind stopping if we see a shaggy dog? You see, he's mine and I'm looking for him."

The man gave William the books to hold and lifted him on to his horse. He was going only a mile along the road to deliver the books to a friend, but he said that William was welcome to have a lift that far. They saw no sign of Bobtail before they reached the house the rider was making for. William slipped down into the road and handed the books back. His new friend looked anxiously at him.

"I expect your dog is home by now. Won't you come in and warm yourself with a drink? You are very wet."

William was going to say no, but he was thirsty and a

cup of warm milk would be very welcome. He followed the man into the yard and waited while he put his horse into a stable and gave him a quick rub down. Then they crossed the yard to the house. The man knocked at the door and they had to wait a long time before it opened.

"Come on, Joseph! Let us in," cried the man. "I have a young friend with me and he is thirsty. You can get him a glass of milk and something a little stronger for myself."

While he waited for his drink, William looked with interest at the untidy piles of books and still more untidy piles of calculations written in crabbed handwriting which littered every available table space in the room. He stared at the other end of the room, where liquids were boiling and bubbling in their glass containers. Was this man a wizard? He seemed just as interesting as the Wise Woman.

William drank his milk and listened to the men's talk, but he couldn't understand it. They were talking about air. William knew all about the Composition of Matter. Parson Blickley had taught him that all matter on this earth was composed of Earth, Air, Fire and Water. Everybody knew that. But this man seemed to be saying that air wasn't just air. He talked about several gases which seemed to be kinds of air.

William watched in wonder as he took a little silk bag and opened it out with his fingers. He held it above one of the boiling liquids and then let it go. Its sides filled out and the whole bag floated to the ceiling and stayed there.

"If I let them see that, I'd be burnt at the stake," said the man. "But one day, men will be honoured for demonstrating such things."

"Is it magic?" asked William.

"No," said the man. "It's science, but most people aren't ready for it." William felt snubbed, so he took his milk to the window and looked out into the street. He was sipping the last of the milk and thinking about leaving, when he heard the scientist say, "Locked in my stable it was. It knocked me clean over and rushed away, leaving me on my back in my own yard. An enormous shaggy brute of a dog."

William rushed up to him. "Where *is* he?" he shouted.

"How should I know?" replied the scientist irritably. "At the rate he was going, he'll be in Bridgwater by now."

13 : The search

Becky woke on Wednesday morning and looked at the empty bed on the other side of the room. It had been late on Monday afternoon when the family realized William was missing. Robert Ashe had called in to tease him for being a sleepy-head, and his absence was discovered. Immediately, Robert Ashe and her father had set out to look for him, but it was already dark, and all they could do was to take lanterns and call William's name across the flooded fields.

It was the floods that were the main worry. Water draining off the surrounding hills collected in drainage ditches on either side of the road, and these were especially deep whenever there had been a lot of rain. The tides were another problem. Although the Garsons lived some way from the sea, the tides sometimes affected them. When there was an extra high tide, more water than usual was pushed up the rivers. The rivers overflowed their banks, and the water flooded across the fields. In the past week, there had been some very high tides, and a great deal of rain. When people went missing at such times, there was always a fear that they had been drowned.

Becky came slowly downstairs. She hated the early morning, with no William and the worried faces of her parents as they began another day without him. First Bobtail and now William. It was all like a bad dream. She came into the kitchen and found her father finishing a meal and her mother packing a bag of provisions. That meant he would be going out again. Nell was asleep, and Watchboy, no longer wearing a splint, was limping unhappily about the room. Becky ran to greet Watchboy, but her eyes were on her father. Where would he go today? Yesterday, neighbours from miles around had come to help. They had taken boats and rowed up and down across the flooded fields and found nothing.

Mr. Garson's eyes were tired as he prepared for a second day of exploring the waters with little hope of finding William alive. There was a knock at the door and Robert Ashe appeared.

"The flood waters are going down," he said. "We'd best take a look and see . . ." He broke off, seeing Mr. Garson's warning glance as he shook his head and indicated Becky.

"William isn't drowned," she cried. She ran to her mother and clung to her, burying her head in her apron.

"No, my precious, of course he isn't," said her mother. "Now stop crying. It won't bring William back any quicker." She turned to the two men. "What are you going to do today?"

"If the floods have gone down, we'll search on foot," said Mr. Garson.

The two men left and Becky wandered miserably round the house, getting in her mother's way. Mrs. Garson set her to make some oatcakes to keep her mind off William. But when Becky burnt them, she sent her away.

Becky went upstairs and sat on the window-seat. She sighed and leant her forehead against the cool pane. If only a miracle would happen and she could see William and Bobtail coming back together along the drove road. Where could William have gone? Had he stumbled on the road in the dark and fallen into the ditch on the way over to Robert Ashe? That was what everyone thought. That was why her father looked so unhappy. He was blaming himself for letting William go alone. He told Robert Ashe that he had got up at half past four on Monday morning to see about an early breakfast for William before he set out. But William had already left the house. That was what really puzzled everybody. Why had William left so early? They supposed that he must have mistaken the time.

Later that morning the two men returned, tired and wet, to report that they had found nothing.

"Where can he be?" asked Mrs. Garson for the hundredth time.

"Could he have run away?" suggested Robert Ashe.

"Why ever should he run away?" Mr. Garson looked puzzled.

"I don't know, but I can't really see William falling into the flood waters. He isn't that sort of boy. He's far too sensible."

The idea of William's running away had set Mrs. Garson thinking.

"He's gone to join the army," she declared. "You heard how he talked to Becky when he came back from London. Exciting, he said it was when he met the soldiers. I knew no good would come of taking him to Smithfield."

"I don't think he would do that," said Mr. Garson. "He's too young, and too much attached to his home."

"William's a brave lad, but he's no soldier," said Robert Ashe. They sat round the table and had a meal, but very little was said.

"We'll have to give those fields another try," said Mr. Garson at last. "The water's gone down a couple of inches since this morning."

They left the house once more and Becky went back to sit at the landing window. She was still there when they returned two hours later. They had taken horses and followed the road to Bridgwater to see if William had been washed down with the waters as they subsided. Mr. Garson's horse had pulled a muscle and was dead lame.

"If I need a horse tomorrow, I shall borrow Parson Blickley's," he said. "Though I've no idea what we shall be doing tomorrow. We've done all we can as it is."

"Parson Blickley!" shouted Becky.

Everyone turned and stared at her. She felt shy when she found them all looking in her direction, but her father's words had reminded her of something. She remembered sitting beside Lady Caroline, trying not to cry while Parson Blickley, in the pulpit above her, preached about the Good Shepherd. That night, in the bedroom, William had talked about the Good Shepherd. He had said something about Watchboy being the ninety-nine. Then he wouldn't say any more.

"It's the Good Shepherd," she explained. "I know where William is. He isn't drowned. He's gone, like the Good Shepherd, you know."

The others clearly did not know. Mrs. Garson even wondered whether William's disappearance had affected Becky's mind.

"He's left the ninety-nine, that's Nell and Watchboy (though he forgot Nell) and has gone after the one that was lost," Becky said impatiently, thinking she was making everything clear. "Like Parson Blickley read in the Bible before his sermon on Sunday."

"The one that is lost?" repeated her father.

"Yes, only in the Bible it's a sheep. But it's Bobtail who's lost and William has gone to find him."

Mr. and Mrs. Garson looked at each other.

"Did he say he was going to look for Bobtail?" asked her father.

"No," said Becky. "But before we went to sleep that night, we were talking about Parson Blickley and the Good Shepherd. At least, William was. And then he went quiet and wouldn't talk and I went to sleep."

"It's a chance," said Mr. Garson. He turned to Robert Ashe. "We'll take fresh horses at once. We'll go all the way to London if necessary. The more I think of it, the more sure I am that the young rascal has gone off to find the pup."

14 : Bobtail in trouble

Bobtail bounded along through the mud and rain in high spirits. He held his precious bone tightly between his teeth, and he panted as he ran, so that his breath hung like a mist around his head. At midday he stopped to rest. He lay on the grass beneath a willow tree, dropped the bone and began to chew it. He had already picked off all the meat and sucked the marrow from its centre. Now it was nothing more than a hollow tube. He ground his teeth over it for a quarter of an hour. Then he scrambled down the bank and had a long drink from the ditch. Back on the road once more, he sniffed at his bone, but left it where it was and walked off without it.

A little later he stopped and sniffed the air excitedly. He had reached a familiar stretch of road. It was still some way from home, but he had often driven cattle along here in the summer with Watchboy. The road ran straight for almost a mile, and then bent sharply to the right, past a large farmhouse. Bobtail trotted confidently along in the middle of the road, slopping through mud which splashed him from head to foot.

In the distance behind him came the noise of galloping hooves, squelching mud and the swish of water. A large coach was coming from Glastonbury, pulled by a pair of high-spirited horses. It was empty, except for the driver, and he was travelling far too quickly for the state of the road. He lashed his horses furiously as he came up behind Bobtail, urging them to gallop even faster. Bobtail leaped to one side as the coach bore down on him. He missed the coach by inches, but ran straight into the path of three horsemen who came round the bend on the road just at that moment.

The horse on the nearside ran off the road and plunged down the bank, taking himself and his rider into the ditch. Somehow, the other two riders managed to wrench their horses' heads round, and avoid a headlong collision with the coach. The coach driver tried to pull up his horses, but the coach was too heavy, and as the horses sank on to their hindquarters it continued to move forward. Fortunately for the animals, its shafts snapped, and it swerved to one side, leaving the horses struggling in the slippery mud. The coach came to a halt at a crazy angle, with its shafts stuck in the mud, and the driver went hurtling through the air to land in a blackthorn bush.

No one spared a thought for Bobtail. He had been kicked by several pairs of iron-shod hooves and lay quite still at the side of the road. Above him a tremendous row had broken out. One man clambered from the ditch, leading his horse. His hair was plastered to his head, and with his free hand he was wiping evil-smelling weed and slime from his face and clothes. He stood on the bank and shouted angrily at the coach driver, who was still hanging helplessly in the blackthorn bush. The other two riders left their horses to go to the assistance of the coach horses, which were partly trapped by the coach.

The coach was too heavy for them and they had to get the driver out of the bush so that he could help them. His horses were a pathetic sight; their eyes rolled wildly as they struggled up and stood trembling and covered with sweat. It seemed a miracle that they were still alive, but the driver was too angry to care whether they were alive or dead. He turned on the horsemen and accused them of causing the accident.

Just then, two servants arrived from the farm. There

were often accidents on this stretch of road, but this was one of the noisiest they had heard. Everyone ranted and raved. Each side blamed the other. The coach driver at last turned to one of the servants and demanded a horse from the farm so that he could continue his journey to Bridgwater. He said that he had important business to do there, which had to be concluded before sundown.

The servant hurried off, and returned with men bringing ropes and six oxen to pull the coach clear, because it was blocking the road. The farmer had come with them. The coach driver rushed towards him, demanding a saddle horse, but the farmer brushed him aside and went straight to the coach horses. He spoke soothingly to them until they were in a fit state to be led away to a stable. Only then would he talk about arrangements for a fresh horse, and payment for the use of his oxen. This set the driver off again. He accused the riders of going too fast, and said that they should bear the cost of the oxen and the hire of his horse.

The argument might have continued all the afternoon, but the coach driver suddenly saw Bobtail lying at the side of the road.

"There's the cause of our trouble," he declared, pointing at the dog. "We shouldn't be here now if it hadn't been for that animal."

They all agreed that it was Bobtail who had caused the accident. The farmer doubted it, but kept quiet. He had not been there at the time, but he knew how fast men rode and drove along this stretch of road. He agreed to find clothes for the wet horseman, as well as a horse for the coach driver, so at last they all went on their way, and the farmer was heartily glad to see them go.

His men stayed behind to harness the ox team to the wreck of the coach and pull it clear. It took them a good hour, with the labouring beasts sinking to their bellies in mud at each step they took. The coach was left at the side of the road and the oxen were led away. One of the men prodded Bobtail with his foot. As he didn't move,

he picked him up and threw him into the ditch before following the others back to the farm.

The shock of the icy water brought Bobtail to his senses. He spluttered as water went up his nose and down his throat, and began to scrabble towards the bank. His long coat dragged him down and his bruised body prevented him from paddling strongly. When he reached the bank, he was too weak to scramble out and had to let himself slip back into the water. Four times he tried to clamber out and four times he slid back. Each attempt to reach dry land was feebler than the last and the effort to hold up his head became more than he could manage. He took in another gulp of water, and came up choking. His body rolled and floated helplessly in the ditch. He managed to keep close to the side, but the steep banks were too much for him.

At last he reached the roots of a willow tree which were growing into the water. He managed to hook a paw over one of the roots and this gave him a breathing space. He coughed up some water, felt better and tried once more to climb out, but it was too painful and his strength began to fail again. He slipped off the root and paddled slowly away. His paw strokes had become very feeble now and his head went under more frequently. His whole body had begun to sink, when he was brought up against a grid of willow stakes which had been set in the bank to stop rubbish passing through a land drain at the side of the ditch.

The bank here had been cut away by the men who had fixed the grid, and Bobtail was at last able to drag his numbed body out of the water. He lay exhausted on the ground and coughed up the water he had swallowed. Then he pulled himself, inch by inch, away from the water, and made for an old willow stump whose gnarled grey trunk was quite hollow. He crept into it and started to curl up into a ball, which was how he kept himself warm on cold nights, but he found he was more comfortable if he stretched out. He couldn't fit all of himself into the tree, so he lay with his head and front paws outside. He lay there, only half conscious, while his body temperature sank lower and lower.

15 : Rescue

William dashed out of the scientist's house and pelted down the road. In no time at all he was splattered with mud from head to foot; the hood of his cloak had fallen back and rain was dripping from his hair into his eyes and down his face. He hardly noticed it. He ran on, hoping against hope that there would still be time to catch up with Bobtail before he reached home. He felt that it would be easier to explain why he had run away if he could return with Bobtail beside him.

After five minutes he had a terrible stitch in his side. It was so bad that he doubled over for a moment to relieve the pain. Then he straightened up and hurried on, half walking and half running, with his hand pressed against his side. After a while, a horseman overtook him and offered him a lift. Gladly, William let himself be swung into the saddle, and sat happily, covering the miles far more quickly than he could have run them. He was put down at last near the straight stretch of road which people living thereabouts called the Long Mile.

He stooped to pick up something lying at the side of the road. It was a hollow marrow bone, and as he examined it, he saw how it was scored at the ends by tooth marks. He rubbed his finger and thumb along its surface, and wondered what sort of dog had left it there. He walked on, holding the bone in his hand. He didn't want to put it down in case those were Bobtail's tooth-marks; he felt the bone was a link between him and his dog. He started to run. Once he got to the Long

Mile, he would have a good view of the road ahead, and he might see Bobtail.

Bobtail wasn't on the straight stretch of road, and William tried not to feel disappointed. He told himself over and over again that Bobtail was safely at home, waiting for him. He hurried on towards the bend in the road ahead. All he wanted to do now, was to reach home himself.

A group of youths, led by an older man, came round the bend towards him, carrying an odd assortment of farm implements. Some had spades, others carried pitchforks and one or two had scythes. The older man was better equipped. He had a sword in his belt and carried a pike in his hand.

William thought they looked very rough, and was glad that the older man was there. He had heard that there were bands of men like this, travelling from the country into the cities to offer their services to the army, in the hope that there was going to be a war. He wondered how far they were going. If they were making for Bristol, they would be on Parliament's side. Bristol was the only city for miles around that supported Parliament. Everywhere else in the West, people were for the King. The group had stopped to examine the wreck of what had been a handsome coach, and William passed them as they were clambering in and out of it. He quickened his pace slightly, pleased that they seemed to be too busy tearing the coach apart to bother with him. But a yellow-haired lad spotted him.

He stepped out of the coach and walked up to William, blocking his way so that he had to stop. William side-stepped in order to get past, and the youth put out a foot and tripped him. William picked himself up and faced his tormentor. By this time, some of the others had climbed down from the coach and were standing around to watch the fun.

"You're going the wrong way," said the yellow-haired lad.

"No I'm not," said William.

"I say you are, because you're coming to Bristol with us," and the youth spun him round to face the way he had come.

"I can't come," said William. "I've got to get home. Farm business," he added, hoping it sounded important.

"All business can wait," said the lad, "except war business."

The older man spoke up. "Leave him alone. He's too young. We don't want children."

But the others were not going to let William off so easily.

"Are you for King or Parliament?" someone asked.

"King," said William stoutly.

"A King's man! We don't want a King's man, do we, fellows?"

"No," they all roared.

"What do we do to a King's man?" asked one of them.

"Drown him," chorused the others.

"Leave him," commanded the man with the pike. "He's a child. Send him home to his mother."

"We'll drown him first," said the yellow-haired youth, and, picking William up, he threw him into the ditch.

The group moved off with yells and hoots of laughter, and William was left to scramble out as best he could.

He looked down at his legs, which were coated with the thick, shiny black mud from the bottom of the ditch. Foul-smelling slime dripped from his head and he wiped it with his cloak. Tears rolled down his face, but they were tears of anger. Bobtail would be home, and here he was in this mess. His teeth chattered uncontrollably as he set himself to run up and down the bank, flinging his arms across his chest in an attempt to get warm.

His legs felt stiff beneath their coat of clammy mud, and he bent down to pick up a stick to scrape some of it off. As he stooped, he noticed that the amulet was no longer swinging from its chain around his neck. That was the last straw. His lucky talisman, the amulet which was to have brought him to Bobtail, had fallen off in his struggle with the boys. He had to find it. He believed in it, and wanted to prove to himself that the Wise Woman had been right. He moved slowly forward, with his eyes on the ground, kicking the grass with his boots, and stooping to look among the tree roots. The amulet was quite heavy, and had probably flown through the air for some way. He moved on until his path was blocked by an old tree. The bottom was hollow and he noticed a piece of dirty grey fur sticking out of it.

"Rabbit," he thought, and went round to investigate.

A lifeless huddle of grey fur lay there, scarcely moving. Then it raised its head, and a blue eye and a brown eye, immensely tired, looked into his. The fur at the end of the spine wagged feebly and a wuff of pleasure came from the dog's throat. Then the head went down and the eyes closed. William threw himself down and gathered Bobtail in his arms. There seemed to be so little life left, as he took off his cloak and wrapped it round the dog. The cloak was soaking wet, but William hoped that it might hold a little of his body warmth, enough to keep Bobtail alive until help came.

He had to get help. It wasn't far away. He knew there was a farm just along the road. "I shan't be long, Bobtail," he said. "Not long." He stood up, prepared to

race to the farm for help, but Bobtail put up a feeble paw to stop him and opened his eyes to look straight into William's.

William felt dreadful. "I've got to leave you. Just for a minute," he said.

Bobtail's paw fell more heavily on his arm. "He doesn't understand," thought William. "I can't explain. I'll have to take him with me."

He pulled at Bobtail, but he was a dead weight, and as William struggled on his own to move him, Bobtail moaned with pain.

"Oh why doesn't someone come?" said William. "Please, somebody come. I can't lift him on my own. What am I going to do?"

A pair of filthy boots appeared beside William and stopped.

"Found him then, have you?"

It was the beggar. If it had been an angel from

heaven, William couldn't have been more pleased to see him.

"Help me," he said.

"You did me a good turn, lad, now it's up to me to do something for you." He lifted Bobtail out of the hollow tree and stood with him in his arms, staggering.

"Now, what would you want me to do with this dog of yours? He won't last long, I reckon."

"We've got to carry him to the farmhouse down the road," said William. "I'll help you."

"No, boy, I can't do that."

"Why ever not?"

"Reckon they don't like me there. You see, there was a couple of ducks . . ."

"I was right to hate you," said William. "You only think of your own skin."

"I has to," said the beggar. "No one else does. I've got your dog out of the tree for you. What else do you want? He's almost gone, anyway."

William stamped his foot. While they were arguing, Bobtail was dying.

"Look, all I want you to do is to help me get Bobtail as far as the road outside the house. You needn't come in."

Grumbling, the man moved off, and walked along the road until they were in sight of the farm. Here he stopped.

"Looks like he's dead, this dog of yours. Now why don't you and me . . ."

"Put my dog down and get out," said William.

The beggar wasn't listening. His ears had caught the sound of approaching horses. "I'm off," he said, and laid Bobtail on the grass.

"Good," said William. "If my dog dies, it'll be your fault for wasting my time."

"Ungrateful young brute," said the beggar angrily,

"I'd like to . . ."

He never finished his threat, because there was a shout from one of the men on horseback.

"William!"

William looked up to see his father and Robert Ashe looking down at him. Mr. Garson reached down and pulled him up on to the saddle. "William, what have you done to yourself?"

"Has this man harmed you?" Robert Ashe was looking angrily at the beggar.

"No," said William. "Some boys pushed me into the ditch. I'm all right, but we must do something about Bobtail."

"I never laid hands on him, sir," whined the beggar, backing away. "I was helping with the dog. He's a good lad. A kind boy to an old man."

"Please DO something for Bobtail," William shouted. Here were three grown-ups all talking, instead of saving his dog's life.

But Mr. Garson acted quickly enough when he saw that William was unhurt. He carried Bobtail into the house, leaving Robert Ashe to take the horses to the stable. William turned to follow his father, but the beggar had him by the shoulders.

"Here, lad. What about something for a poor old man? That's a valuable dog, I can see."

William tried to pull himself away, but the beggar held on to him, demanding payment.

"Pay you!" yelled William. "You took my guinea. Pay you? I'll tell them about the ducks and the goose. Let me go. I want to see if Bobtail's still alive." He kicked the beggar's shins and bit his hand. It tasted horrible, but the man let William go.

"You little firebrand. I'd lift another guinea off you for that, I would."

"So you did take it," said William, and ran into the

farmyard, while the beggar chuckled and ambled off down the road.

William found his way to the great farmhouse kitchen, where Bobtail was lying on a pile of sacks in front of the fire. His father was bending over him and pouring something from a flask down Bobtail's throat. William pushed past everyone and knelt beside Bobtail.

"Is he going to be all right?"

"I'm not sure." Mr. Garson lifted one of Bobtail's eyelids and let it drop again. He passed his hands carefully all over the dog's body. "There's very little outward damage," he said. "I think he's very badly bruised. But worst of all, he's far too cold. When an animal gets as cold as he is . . ." He shook his head. "We must just keep hoping."

In spite of himself, William began to shiver violently. He had been so worried about Bobtail that he had forgotten how cold he was himself, and nobody else seemed to have noticed.

But it was the first thing the farmer's wife noticed when she came into the room. In no time at all she had carried William away to strip off his wet things. William resisted. He wanted to be with Bobtail. So she placed an enormous tub of hot water in front of the fire beside Bobtail and put William in it.

"Bless the pair of them," she said. "They can thaw out together."

William lay in the hot water, watching anxiously as Robert Ashe and his father worked on Bobtail, trying to coax the warmth back into his frozen body. Gradually Bobtail stopped shivering, and they could see the tenseness go out of him as his body temperature returned to normal. His coat steamed as he lay there facing the fire, limp, relaxed and content. He stretched his legs, gave a grunt of pure happiness, and raised his head without effort to look at everybody. His gaze rested longest on

William, who jumped out of the tub, scattering water everywhere, and lay down wet and naked against Bobtail. He put his arms round him, and the pair of them relaxed in the comforting warmth of the flames.

A sudden thought struck William as he lay there. "I never found my amulet," he said, "but the Wise Woman was right. It *did* bring me and Bobtail together after all." And he fell asleep on the sacks, his head in Bobtail's fur.